Schoolmaster to a Nation

William Holmes McGuffey
1800 - 1873

Walnut secretary and other furnitures which belonged to William Holmes McGuffey, now on display in the McGuffey Museum, Miami University Library. Miami University, Oxford, Ohio.

McGuffey

AND HIS READERS

PIETY, MORALITY, AND EDUCATION IN NINETEENTH-CENTURY AMERICA

John H. Westerhoff III

Mott Media
Milford, Michigan

Dedicated
to
Barnie, my wife,
companion, helper, lover,
and friend

McGUFFEY AND HIS READERS

Library of Congress Cataloging in Publication Data

WESTERHOFF, JOHN H.
  McGuffey and his readers.
  1. Readers—History and criticism. 2. McGuffey, William Holmes,
1800-1873. 3. Educators—United States—Biography. 4. United
States—Civilization—19th century. I. Title.
PE1117.M23W4   370'.92'4   77-23989
ISBN 0-88062-006-4

Robert Burkett, Editor

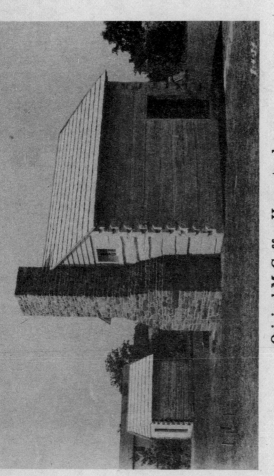

Original McGuffey Homestead
(Eastern Ohio Territory)
Photograph courtesy of Miami University, Oxford, Ohio

William Holmes McGuffey home in Oxford, Ohio
(Today it houses the McGuffey Museum)
Photograph courtesy of Miami University, Oxford, Ohio

Alexander Hamilton McGuffey
(Author of the Fifth Reader
and the Eclectic Speller)

Unique eight-sided desk created by McGuffey
(it rotated on its pedestal)
Photograph courtesy of Miami University, Oxford, Ohio

CONTENTS

PREFACE

The subject of this book was introduced to me by Robert Wood Lynn, onetime Auburn Professor of Religion and Education at Union Theological Seminary in New York and presently on the staff of the Lilly Foundation. The research and portions of the content in this book first appeared as an Ed.D. dissertation at Columbia University Teacher's College in 1975: "William Holmes McGuffey: Studies on the World-View and Value System in the First Editions of the *Eclectic First, Second, Third,* and *Fourth Readers.*" Professors Robert Lynn, Philip Phenix, Douglas Sloan, Dwayne Huebner, and President Lawrence Cremin continually guided me with constructive criticism and personal support; without their aid this book would never have been written. I trust that its contribution to the history of education in the United States will be equal to their confidence and encouragement. Further I would like to express my debt to Miami University in Oxford, Ohio, especially Helen Ball, special collection librarian, and Sterling Cook, curator of the McGuffey Museum; without their cooperation and assistance, this book could never have been completed.

Inside the McGuffey Museum
Oxford, Ohio
Photograph courtesy of Miami University, Oxford, Ohio

Old Engraving Tools
McGuffey Museum
Photograph courtesy of Miami University, Oxford, Ohio

CHAPTER I

Schoolmaster for the Nation?

William Holmes McGuffey—born September 23, 1800, on the Ohio frontier, died May 4, 1873, at Charlottesville, Virginia—was continuing to make the news in 1976, the nation's bicentennial year. For many common folk, McGuffey represents the most important figure in the history of American public education—*the* schoolmaster of the nation!

At his death the National Education Association passed a resolution:

> In the death of William H. McGuffey, late Professor of Moral Philosophy in the University of Virginia, this Association feels that they have lost one of the great lights of the profession whose life was a lesson full of instruction; an example and model to American teachers.
>
> His labors in the cause of education, extending over a period of half a century, in several offices as teacher of common schools, college professor and college president, and as author of text-books; his almost unequaled industry; his power in the lecture room; his influence upon his pupils and community; his care for the public interests of education; his lofty devotion to duty; his conscientious Christian

character—all these have made him one of the noblest ornaments of our profession in this age, and entitle him to the grateful remembrance of this Association and of the teachers of America. (Elmira, New York, August 7, 1873)

Now a century later, the cry "Back to McGuffey's Readers" is heard almost as frequently as "Back to the Bible." Among the masses of Americans, the names of few educators have endured as long as his. Nevertheless, McGuffey has been typically ignored by historians. For example, in his *Oxford History of the American People* Samuel Eliot Morison lauds seven nineteenth-century persons for their contributions to education: Horace Mann, chairman of the Massachusetts Board of Education; Victor Cousin, author of a report on Prussian education; Calvin Stowe, author of a report on education in Europe; Orville H. Browning, Illinois educator and friend of the common school movement; George Ticknor, Harvard professor and leader of the movement to make higher education more varied and flexible; and James Gordon Bennett and Horace Greeley, New York newspapermen who were advocates of public education.[1] While few, if any, of these names are even recognizable by the general population, the name of W. H. McGuffey, remembered fondly by a host of common folk, is significantly missing.

William Holmes McGuffey—clergyman, professor of ancient languages and philosophy, college president, advocate of public education, and textbook compiler—represents an anomaly in history. He remains one of those persons whose influence is still testified to by great numbers of average citizens, but whose life and work are more often than not neglected or shunned by scholars.

Generally unmentioned by historians of culture and only peripherally by historians of education, McGuffey nevertheless gave his name to one of the most remarkable educational ventures of the nineteenth century. It is estimated that at least 120 million copies of McGuffey's Readers were sold between 1836 and 1920, placing their sales in a class with the Bible and Webster's Dictionary.

Indeed, since 1961 they have continued to sell at a rate of some thirty thousand copies a year.[2] No other textbooks bearing a single person's name have approached that mark.

Among the first schoolbooks originating on the midwestern frontier in the period that marked the birth of both America's national consciousness and the common school movement, McGuffey's Readers sold over seven million copies before 1850 and by 1890 had become the basic school readers in thirty-seven states.[3] More amazing, they are still in use in some school systems, and although controversial, they continue to be the desired text of numerous parents' groups who are dissatisfied with modern American education.

The name of William H. McGuffey is recorded in the "people's" educational hall of fame, and the Readers that bear his name have without a doubt influenced American history. In 1928 Henry Ford personally issued a reprint of the six McGuffey Readers (the 1857 edition), which he nostalgically remembered as significant in his own education. At that time he wrote:

> Most youngsters of my day were brought up on the *McGuffey Readers*. Most of those youngsters who still survive have a profound respect for the compiler of the *Readers*. The moral principles Dr. William Holmes McGuffey stressed, the solid character building qualities he emphasized, are stressed and emphasized . . . today even though the *McGuffey Readers* themselves are not "required reading."[4]

In a *Saturday Evening Post* article entitled "That Guy McGuffey," Hugh Fullerton made the claim that, with the exception of the Bible, McGuffey's Readers represent the most significant force in the framing of our national morals and tastes.

> For seventy-five years his [McGuffey's] system and his books guided the minds of four-fifths of the school children of the nation in their taste for literature, in their morality, in their social development and next to the Bible in their religion.[5]

Earlier, Ralph Rush had noted in *The Literature of the Middle Western Frontier:*

> Upon the generations immediately succeeding the pioneer period the influence of McGuffey may well have been greater than that of any other writer or statesman in the West. His name has become a tradition not yet extinct.[6]

It was such convictions, repeated countless times, that prompted Mark Sullivan in 1929 to chastise historians and scholars for ignoring McGuffey, the "most popular, most affectionately remembered person in the nineteenth century, a national giant to be ranked with George Washington and Abraham Lincoln."[7]

Nevertheless, through the years only a few academics have chosen to remember "the masses' teacher."[8] Recently, however, numerous additional claims have been advanced to support the significance of McGuffey and his Readers for the history of American religion and education. For example, Henry Steele Commager wrote of the Readers: "They played an important role in American education . . . and helped to shape that elusive thing we call the American character."[9] Charles Carpenter commented: "It has been recognized by students of history that the lessons in the McGuffey Readers did much to set the standards of morality and of the social life in the pioneering West for more than a century."[10] John Nietz remarked: "The readers fitted in appropriately with their time. They were essentially in step with the era in which they were published."[11]

In his important essay, "Civil Catechetics in Mid-Victorian America," Robert Wood Lynn commented upon the commitment to civil religion that has moved successive generations of Protestants—from the first New England Puritans to the progressive religious educators in the early 1900s—to launch an impressive variety of educational enterprises. Lynn contended that McGuffey's Readers were "more than a textbook . . . they were a portable school for the new priests of the republic." Lynn reminded us that in the experience of many Americans growing up along the

Middle Border in the later part of the nineteenth century, McGuffey was quite literally the "lord of the mystery called education." McGuffey's Readers, he wrote, "embodied a vision of piety, justice and the commonwealth, a form of 'patriotic piety' which still appeals to some folk living amidst our current 'crisis of loyalty.'" [12]

Still, while new acknowledgments of McGuffey's importance to American educational history have been made and numerous claims advanced as to the significance of McGuffey's Readers, we know little about either McGuffey or his Readers. Surely both deserve more scholarly attention than they have been given; for despite the works mentioned and a comparatively few doctoral dissertations, the most "famous and influential" textbooks in the annals of American educational history have not received the objective study they deserve. [13]

McGuffey's Readers vs. McGuffey

The influence of William H. McGuffey must be distinguished from the influence of McGuffey's Readers. McGuffey was responsible for the compilation of the first four Readers, but not for the fifth or sixth, which were compiled by his brother Alexander. Furthermore, McGuffey compiled the 1836–37 edition of the Reader, but he was not responsible for any edition after 1857. These facts present us with serious problems because most commentaries on McGuffey's Readers have depended on lessons found in the later (1857 and 1879) editions of the Readers and content primarily from the Fourth, Fifth, and Sixth Readers. [14] More important is the realization that numerous significant changes were made by the various editors of the series, the most dramatic changes being found in the 1857 and the 1879 editions. While McGuffey's name continued to be carried on these radically revised editions, he neither contributed to them nor approved their content. To depend on material from these sources may be legitimate for understanding McGuffey's Readers, but not for understanding William

Holmes McGuffey or the Readers he personally compiled. Although McGuffey has been rediscovered as a major figure in American religious, educational, and social history, an exploration of his life and an investigation of his thought as revealed in his writings and the Readers he compiled is still needed.

Historical Significance

Two of the best-known schoolbooks in the history of American education were the eighteenth-century's *New England Primer* and the nineteenth-century's McGuffey's Readers. Of these two, McGuffey's Readers were both the most popular and the most widely used.[15] In chapter 3 we will summarize the world view and value system in the first editions of the *Eclectic First*, *Second*, *Third*, and *Fourth Readers* compiled by William Holmes McGuffey in 1836–37.

On the basis of McGuffey's life history, his writings, and his personally compiled Readers, it is reasonable to say that he was a theological and pedagogical conservative. He understood the purpose of public schooling in terms of moral and spiritual education, and he sought to provide the school with a curriculum that would nurture persons in Presbyterian Calvinist understandings and ways. Such purposes and aims were perhaps noble and somewhat a mirror of early nineteenth-century America, but they were not suited to the nation's later need for a unified pluralism. Therefore the content of the Readers radically changed between the 1836–37 edition McGuffey compiled for Truman and Smith and the 1879 revised edition Henry Vail edited and compiled for Van Antwerp, Bragg and Company. This edition is still published by the American Book Company under a 1920 copyright by Henry Vail and still used in more schools than might be imagined.

While these two major editions (the first in 1836–37 and the last in 1879) share some content in common, they are significantly more different than alike. McGuffey, who died in 1873, more than likely would not have approved of the changes made in this later edition.

By 1879, the theistic, Calvinist world view so dominant in the first editions had disappeared, and the prominent values of salvation, righteousness, and piety were entirely missing. All that remained were lessons affirming the morality and life-styles of the emerging middle class and those cultural beliefs, attitudes, and values that undergird American civil religion.

In general, the 1879 revised edition of *McGuffey's Eclectic Readers* were compiled to meet the needs of national unity and the dream of a "melting pot" for the world's oppressed masses. Their lessons were especially appropriate for a small-town, rural population that experienced stable, semi-extended family life, minimal mobility, and a simple life-style.

While a few continuations of the concerns dominant in the 1836–37 editions remain (such as kindness and patriotism), the contents of the 1879 edition have been severely secularized. Calvinistic theology and ethics have been replaced by American middle-class civil religion, morality, and values. Nevertheless, for those who deplore the urbanization, secularism, social and ethnic pluralism, situation ethics, and prophetic character of schoolbooks of today, this 1879 edition of McGuffey's Readers seems like a breath of fresh air, a blessing from God. While a long way from the values McGuffey sought to pass on to the next generation, each new edition continued to introduce students to the classics, to morality, and to a good character as understood by the emerging middle class. They encouraged the development of the intellect and gave children a cosmopolitan view of life. Most important, they offered our nation's children common experiences, knowledge, and frame of reference; indeed, they strove to unify the nation around a common world view and value system. They are more than a historical curiosity. McGuffey's Readers played an important role in America's history, and in retrospect their contribution was positive.

It is important to realize, however, that there are three distinct editions of McGuffey Readers—1836–37, 1857, and 1879—each compiled by a new editor, for a new publisher, to meet new needs. Only the name of the Readers is historically continuous. William H. McGuffey is therefore best understood as a representative of an era's end, a transition point in the history of religion and education. His personally compiled Readers provide us with an example of public school curriculum in the first half of the nineteenth century, before the common school movement significantly took hold. Indeed, the history of the Reader's various editions is best understood as a mirror of changes occurring in the history of American public education and as a demonstration of the marketing know-how of textbook publishers to meet the changing demands of the nation's schools. Still, the first editions of McGuffey's Readers provide us with an important indicator of the world view and value system of Scotch Presbyterians and other Protestants on the American frontier during the first half of the nineteenth century, cultural understandings and ways that did not significantly influence the later history of American public education. In any case, it would be difficult to understand our nation's history without understanding W. H. McGuffey and the Readers he compiled for our frontier schools at the beginning of the nineteenth century.

McGuffey's Influence

Obviously, McGuffey's Readers were not the only schoolbooks used in the 1800s. In fact, there were a number of other successful readers published during the period in which McGuffey's Readers reigned. *Sanders' Readers* by Charles Sanders, *The University Series* by George Holmes, *The Appleton Readers* by William Torrey Harris, and *The Hillard Readers* represent four nineteenth-century series that might be compared with McGuffey's Readers.

Because of conclusions reached by Ruth Elson in *Guardians of Tradition*, a content comparison between these various schoolbooks could prove to be important for historians of education. For example, Elson comments at length on racism and anti-Semitism in nineteenth-century textbooks.[16] Interestingly, children using the 1836–37 editions of McGuffey's Readers would not have been aware that there were blacks or Jews nor, for that matter, would they have been aware that there was slavery or any other social problem, though there were poor individuals in need of charity. It appears that only in later editions of McGuffey's Readers did such concerns and issues appear.[17]

Further, the 1836–37 editions of McGuffey's Readers seem to be more cosmopolitan in their use of heroes, more benevolent toward American Indians, more theological in content, and more concerned about salvation and piety than any other schoolbooks of the period. Considering that McGuffey compiled his Readers from existing schoolbooks, their uniqueness provides us with important indicators, not only of the unusual character of the first editions of his Readers, but also of the intention with which he compiled their contents.

It seems clear that W. H. McGuffey communicated his own unique frontier Presbyterian world view and value system through the compilation of his Readers. Schools will always reflect the understandings and values of the society at large. Education necessarily deals with piety and morality, in one way or another, but if our schools and schoolbooks have changed, it is because the nation has changed. McGuffey spoke to his time and place. Indeed, his Readers were truly unequaled in mirroring late eighteenth-century thought. But they did not seem to represent the emerging needs of the second half of the nineteenth century. Still McGuffey's important first editions influenced the 1857 and 1879 editions to speak to their time and place. So it is, that while the first editions were simply called *Eclectic Readers*, by 1841 McGuffey had become so famous that the publisher decided to call them *McGuffey's Eclectic Readers*. McGuffey's name rightly is remembered as a major contributor to the history of

American public education and the history of American schoolbooks.

The Readers and the Public Schools

What do Americans expect of their public schools? Reading, writing, and arithmetic, surely, but much more. For most of the two hundred years of America's national life, schools have been expected to instill piety, mold character, and transmit community values. By the second quarter of the nineteenth century it was argued that it was the public responsibility to provide both formal instruction and moral education in schools that were free, publicly subsidized, and publicly controlled. The new public school had weighty responsibilities. It was expected to instill patriotism, develop civic responsibility, assimilate newcomers into the majority culture, provide occupational training, and produce an educated citizenry essential to a democracy. Perhaps even more important was the responsibility of creating a unified pluralism within our nation.

Beginning with Massachusetts in 1852 and ending with Mississippi in 1918, every state in the Union decided to require children to attend school. The goal of national unity was to be dependent upon the centrality of schooling and the uniformity of learning. If the nation, following the Civil War, was to have a personality founded upon common moral principles and a common will, a shared ideology and set of values needed to be sustained and transmitted. The purpose of compulsory education sought to contribute to this standardized pattern of institutional learning, and the schoolbook became the school's most important resource for meeting its calling.

Textbook publishers, of course, desired the largest possible market, but they also shared the purposes of America's emerging public schools and therefore sought to provide textbooks to meet the emerging needs of the nation's schools. As early as 1837, advertisements claim that McGuffey's Readers were neither sectarian nor sectional. While the first editions of McGuffey's Readers could legitimately be accused of both, it seems that later editions made good on these earlier claims. More interesting, perhaps, is a publisher's controversy that surfaced shortly after the Readers first appeared. William H. More and Company of Cincinnati, publishers of the *Sanders' Readers*, an eastern series reproduced and sold in the West, issued an educational periodical, the *Western School Journal*. As early as 1847, before any major revisions had been made in McGuffey's Readers, they raised questions about the appropriateness of the religious and moral teachings in the Readers. Writers in the *Western School Journal* agreed that school readers had a dual purpose to teach English and morals, but they accused McGuffey of eliminating important religious principles from his books so as to make them more acceptable to Catholics.[18] It appears as if the 1836–37 edition of McGuffey's Readers, while being sectarian, were more ecumenical than some thought wise.

The importance, however, of both this controversy and the publisher's claim of the ecumenical content in their schoolbooks indicates some of the issues facing the public schools. With a growing awareness of pluralism in American society and an awareness of the need for a civil piety and morality, both to hold the nation together and provide it with an identity, the public schools assumed a new and important function. The question emerges, To what extent did the Readers compiled by McGuffey meet this need? The first editions of McGuffey's Readers, while expressing the values and understandings of many, appear to have been an inadequate response to the needs of the day, and therefore the Readers had to be radically changed during the ensuing years if they were to maintain their popularity.

The history of the McGuffey's Readers, therefore, provides us with a guide to what was occurring both in the public school movement and in American culture, for it seems that the contents of the first editions of the Readers became increasingly inappropriate. Conceivably, the Readers compiled by McGuffey, which sold only seven million copies in comparison to the more than sixty million sold of the 1879 edition, may have been the last witness to the orthodoxy of the nation's religious past. Twentieth-century secularism may well have its root in our nineteenth-century public schools. Perhaps the revised editions of the McGuffey's Readers contributed to the emerging goals of the common school, but then left to the churches and their Sunday schools the religious education McGuffey thought important to perpetuate.

W. H. McGuffey, maintaining the inseparability of morality and religion, provides us, in his Readers, with a Presbyterian theistic world view and a religious value system. But the purposes and goals of the United States and its public schools did not share his sectarian views. Perhaps McGuffey's contribution to the history of religion and education is his mirroring of the past more than his molding of the future.

Still the Readers McGuffey compiled remain an important and not fully tapped resource for understanding our national and educational history. In the following chapters we attempt to provide a historically accurate biography of William H. McGuffey, a summary of the content in the first editions of McGuffey's personally compiled editions of the Eclectic Readers, samples of the most typical contents of the 1836–37 editions of the Readers, and the most significant other literary contributions of McGuffey to American education.

William Holmes McGuffey rates a significant place in the history of American public education. Too little is known of his life and work. That void needs to be corrected, and an accurate understanding of this nineteenth-century schoolman and his Readers' contribution to piety, morality, and education revealed.

Notes

1. Samuel Eliot Morison, *Oxford History of the American People* (New York: Oxford University Press, 1965), p. vi.

2. John Nietz, *Old Textbooks* (Pittsburgh: University of Pittsburgh Press, 1961), p. 73.

3. John L. Clifton, *Ten Famous American Educators* (Columbus, Ga.: R. G. Adams & Co., 1933), p. 75.

4. Henry Ford, "The McGuffey Readers," *Colophon*, new series 1, no. 4: 587.

5. Hugh Fullerton, "That Guy McGuffey," *Saturday Evening Post*, November 26, 1927.

6. Ralph Rusk, *The Literature of the Middle Western Frontier* (New York: Columbia University Press, 1925), p. 268.

7. Mark Sullivan, *Our Times* (New York: Scribner's, 1929), p. 11.

8. Now out of print, two of the most frequently quoted books written about McGuffey and his Readers are *A History of the McGuffey Readers* (Cleveland: Burrows Co., 1911) by Henry Vail, onetime editor of the McGuffey Readers, and *William Holmes McGuffey and His Readers* (New York: American Book Co., 1936) by Harvey C. Minnich, onetime professor of education, dean and curator of the McGuffey Museum at Miami University, Oxford, Ohio. For years these basically undocumented works were relied upon as authoritative sources for understanding McGuffey and his Readers. Richard Mosier published *Making the American Mind* (New York: Russell & Russell, 1947), the first major study of McGuffey's thought and its influence on American history. Three years later Alice McGuffey Ruggles, great-granddaughter of William's brother Alexander, penned a new popular biography, *The Story of the McGuffeys* (New York: American Book Co., 1950).

9. Henry Steele Commager, *The Commonwealth of Learning* (New York: Harper, 1962).

10. Charles Carpenter, *History of American Schoolbooks* (Philadelphia: University of Pennsylvania Press, 1963), p. 85.

11. Nietz, *Old Textbooks*, p. 78.

12. Robert Wood Lynn, "Civil Catechetics in Mid-Victorian America: Some Notes about American Civil Religion, Past and Present," *Religious Education*, January-February, 1973, pp. 23, 10, 9.

13. John H. Dawson, "A Survey of Religious Content of Textbooks Written Prior to 1900" (Ph.D. diss., University of Pittsburgh, 1954); Madison Perkins, "Historical Development of the Moral Element in American School Readers" (Ph.D. diss., University of Chicago, 1921); Raymond D. Hughes, "An Analysis of the *Fourth, Fifth*, and *Sixth McGuffey Readers*" (Ph.D. diss., University of Pittsburgh, 1943); James A. Scully, "A Biography of William Holmes McGuffey" (Ph.D. diss., University of Cincinnati, 1967). Other dissertations on McGuffey's Readers listed in the *Comprehensive Dissertation Index 1861-1972*, vol. 22, Xerox University Microfilm: Clarence Richard Causey, "A Comparative Study of the Reading Difficulty of Selected Social Studies Textbooks and the McGuffey Eclectic Readers" (Ed.D. diss., Auburn University, 1971); Walter Haure Hollins, "A Comparative Content Analysis of a Sample of McGuffey and Modern Elementary School Readers" (Ph.D. diss., University of Illinois, Urbana-Campaign, 1959).

14. Even Ruth Miller Elson's *Guardians of Tradition* (Lincoln: University of Nebraska Press, 1964), the most systematic study of American schoolbooks in the nineteenth century, made only some thirty references to McGuffey's Readers, and most of these were chosen from material in the later editions of the Fourth, Fifth, and Sixth Readers. Elson's work, therefore, sheds a minimum of documented light on the mind and spirit of McGuffey or on the first editions of his Readers.

Richard Mosier's *Making the American Mind* remains the major study of the social and moral ideas in McGuffey's Readers. Mosier, who began his work with the assumption that "there is indeed a direct and intimate relation between the curriculum and the culture which students of American civilization have only recently come to investigate" (p. v), sought to interface American cultural history in the nineteenth century with the social and moral ideas contained in McGuffey's Readers. By laying the pattern of ideas he found in the Readers against a background of American thought and culture, Mosier attempted to unveil those ideas and values in American culture that the Readers sought to conserve, defend, and perpetuate. In chapters "The Struggle for Political Power," "Patterns of Nationalism and Patriotism," "Religion and the Conservative Tradition," "The Morality of the Middle Class," and "The Social Virtues," he interwove selected content from various editions of McGuffey's Readers and other historical material on the moral and social conduct of nineteenth-century America.

Acknowledging the significance of Mosier's work, it is nevertheless difficult to determine the extent to which Mosier's understandings of nineteenth-century American life and thought influenced his findings in McGuffey's Readers. Furthermore, Mosier's choice of material to be studied creates some difficulty for understanding McGuffey and his influence on American history. Mosier's investigation claims to include all six Readers in every edition. It is interesting to note, however, that out of his nine hundred references to the Readers, fewer than one hundred (8 percent) come from the first four Readers (seventy from the Fourth, ten from the Third, and seven from the First and Second), and more important, most of these references come from editions published after 1850. For all intents and purposes, then, Mosier neglected the work of William Holmes McGuffey.

While it may have been wise for Mosier to rely on the older editions of the upper-grade Readers—surely they were the most popular and perhaps most influential editions—that decision makes it difficult, if not impossible, to use *Making the American Mind* as a resource for understanding W. H. McGuffey.

15. Carpenter, *History of American Schoolbooks*, p. 85.
16. Elson, *Guardians of Tradition*, p. 67.
17. W. H. McGuffey, *McGuffey's Eclectic Fifth Reader* (Cincinnati: Sargent, Wilson & Hinkle, 1866), pp. 280-82.
18. "Sanders' Readers," *Western School Journal*, March, 1847, p. 39.

CHAPTER II

Biographical Reflections

Each of us to some extent is both a product and a producer of our culture. We cannot entirely separate ourselves from our cultural heritage. To know the understandings and ways of parents and grandparents is to discern aspects of a person's life otherwise inexplicable. Memories, desires, passions, imaginations, understandings, and ways of perceiving and living are passed on to us in ways we do not choose, in ways so rich with life and history that they lie far beyond our consciousness.

An exploration of W. H. McGuffey's generational roots is extremely difficult. Extensive family records are nonexistent, but the few we have, along with family Bibles, township records, and historical knowledge, provide enough clues for a fragile outline of McGuffey's cultural inheritance.

Out of a shadowy past somewhere in the lowlands of Scotland emerges a farmer-cobbler named Billy McGuffey and his wife, Ann McKittrick, both ardent in the faith of the Scottish Covenanters. They lived to witness the passage of

the infamous Enclosure Acts, which took away from the
yeoman class their "commons" where, from time immemo-
rial, they had raised crops, pastured their flock, and
gathered firewood. Responses to this legislation differed
among the people. Some chose to become "servants" of
landlords, others turned to the city for work in newly
emerging factories, while still others sought after a new life
in the New World. Choosing the last, in the spring of 1774,
Billy, thirty-two, and Ann, twenty-seven, and their three
children—Alexander, nicknamed "Sandy," seven;
Catherine, six; and Elizabeth, four—left Wigstone Gallow-
shire, Scotland, and sailed for Philadelphia. After three
months of hardship at sea they landed and soon joined a
community of Scotch-Irish immigrants in York County, on
the southeastern Pennsylvania frontier. There they purchased land for a small farm and, in the spring of 1775,
planted their first crop. Before the first fruits of their labors
could be seen, war was declared with Great Britain.
Leaving his wife and children behind to work the farm, Billy
shouldered his musket and marched away with his
neighbors to fight for the freedom of their new homeland.

For the next seven years, Ann cared for the farm and
reared her children. By the time Billy returned home in
1783, Alexander was a young man. The war had ended, but
the McGuffeys' problems had not. Billy was behind in
payments on his land, and the new, struggling government
of the United States could not reimburse him for his
services.

In 1789 the government announced that cheap land on the
expanding frontier was available to settlers. The pos-
sibilities were attractive, especially since twenty years
earlier a small group of Scotch Covenanters had established
a religious community in Washington County on the
western fringe of Pennsylvania and bound themselves
together in a covenant:

> We, and each of us, whose names are underwritten, being
> chiefly the inhabitants of the western frontier of Washington
> County, considering the many abounding evils in our own

hearts and lives, as also the open and secret violation of the holy law of God, which dishonors His name and defiles and ruins our country; . . . provoking God to send down heavy judgments on our land and to withhold or give His gracious presence, and unfit our soul for enjoying any social happiness, which we desire to acknowledge with shame and sorrow of heart before God, and so in the strength of God and depending on His Grace for support, solemnly promise to engage against both in ourselves and others, as providence shall give opportunity and prudence direct.[1]

Enticed by the opportunity for a new beginning, encouraged by Alexander's restless thirst for adventure, and secure in the knowledge that a community of like-minded folk had preceded them, Billy McGuffey sold his farm and bought land amidst these Scotch-Irish Presbyterian immigrants who had two decades before sought their "promised land" in western Pennsylvania.

At Wheeling Creek in Washington County, Alexander, now twenty-two, helped his father establish a homestead. During these years, a new friend, Duncan McArthur, played an important role in Alexander's life. Although Duncan was three years younger, he had migrated to the area nine years earlier. He influenced Alexander to volunteer with him for service as a scout in the Indian wars.

Five years later, in 1794, a treaty was reached with the Indians, and Duncan and Alexander returned home. Shortly thereafter Duncan married and moved to the Ohio frontier. Three years later, Alexander married Anna Holmes and settled at her family's farm some two miles from the McGuffeys' homestead.

Tradition suggests that the Holmeses were comparatively well-educated, cultured, and wealthy. Their four-hundred-acre farm was the largest in the county; their two-story home with its bookshelf containing six books was atypical. Anna's father was English; her mother Irish. It is said that Anna was a strong, serious, pious, intelligent, literate woman, and Alexander, a fearless, adventurous, disciplined, hard-working, illiterate man. For the next four years Alexander helped his father-in-law tend the farm.

During that time, Anna gave birth to three children. The second child (in a family later to number eleven) was a son, born September 23, 1800, whom they named William after Alexander's father and Holmes after Anna's family.

That is all we know about the family into which William H. McGuffey was born. It is a sparse history, and not completely verifiable, but one that surely played some role in his growth and development. W. H. McGuffey was the product of families who, during the last quarter of the eighteenth century, migrated to the New World, establishing farms in ethnic religious communities, bringing with them a love of God and a belief in education. They were pious pioneer farmers who survived the hardship of the frontier. Who can doubt that they were also adventurous, courageous, disciplined, industrious, and resourceful folk?

Early Child Rearing

Every society provides some means to nurture its young. Most often this socializing institution is the family. Vital to the transmission of culture, the family provides the first, most intimate, and most pervasive element in the formation of character. To understand William Holmes McGuffey is to explore, as best we can, the limited records of his early life.

For the first four years of their marriage, Alexander and Anna lived with Anna's family and worked their farm. When William was two, his family left the comparative comforts of relatives, friends, and the Scotch-Irish community—its churches, stores, and schools—to travel by horseback into a new, lonely, unsettled territory the government had opened to settlers in the wilderness of Trumbull county, the Western Reserve area of Ohio. There on 160 wooded acres they built a log cabin, cleared the land, and established a small farm. In this new homestead, William's parents had five additional children, four girls and a boy.

William was nurtured on the emerging frontier. One can suppose that his life was marked by all the hardships incident to the lot of settlers at the turn of the century. His life more than likely revolved around his family and its struggle for existence. Without nearby schools, churches, and other centers of community and shared nurture, his parents must have played a particularly significant role in his life.

There is no reason to believe that William's childhood was any different from that of others on the frontier. As the eldest son, he surely shared hours of labor at his father's side and assumed many of the same responsibilities as other young men reared on frontier farms. Nevertheless, it is interesting to note that William's father is rarely mentioned. His father's influence, whatever it might have been, is lost in the past. His mother's influence is a different matter. She is the focus of all biographies. William's earliest years were spent in the security and culture of the Holmes household. In his most impressionable years he was provided with an extended family, characterized by piety, learning, and civility. Since he was only two years old when his family migrated to the frontier, the rest of his early childhood was likely to have been spent predominantly at his mother's side. All William's biographers make a point of Anna's dominance in the McGuffey household. Still we know little or nothing about either of William's parents or their frontier life.

Tradition suggests that William's demonstrated love of learning was a result of his mother's influence and teaching. For many children on the frontier, opportunities for schooling were scarce. Inasmuch as education is not merely schooling, or even learning to read and write, much of the education of young people on the frontier came from sources other than schoolrooms and books. We know little about William's socialization, but we do know that he had opportunities many others on the frontier were denied and that schooling played a particularly significant role in his growth and development. For example, school provided him with alternative role models and a variety of experiences radically different from those of most frontier youth.

Thus he learned new skills and acquired new interests that made possible a life different from that of his father and grandfather.

Schooling

Most of the early records of William's life, up to the time when he became a professor at Miami University, concern the schools that he attended and the ministers with whom he lived.

In 1800, the year of William's birth, the Reverend William Wick established the first church in the vicinity of the McGuffeys' farm, at Youngstown. Attending Wick's subscription school, six miles from his home, was one of William's earliest experiences. Wick was a well-educated Calvinist Presbyterian of English descent.[2] William not only studied with Wick but during the winter months lived with the Wick family. During the rest of the year William helped to work the family farm and continued his studies at home. Often after work on the farm he would hike to Wick's home to recite his lessons and to borrow another book that, at his mother's side, he would read late into the night by the light of the fire.[3]

Mr. Wick, like other frontier ministers of the day, had graduated from Canonsburg, a frontier academy, and in preparation for ordination had read theology with a local Presbyterian minister. Almost immediately after his ordination he founded a church and opened a school; for with Scotch Presbyterians, religion and education went together. In such schools, children learned to read, write, and cipher. The instructions and the discipline were harsh, crude, and direct.[4] While we know little about Mr. Wick's school we may indeed ponder McGuffey's enthusiasm. Before William's fourteenth birthday, Mr. Wick is reported to have given William a certificate and advised him that he was ready to become a roving teacher.

So it was that Master McGuffey, at the age of fourteen, agreed to "hold a four-month session of school on lot 4, West

Union" (now Calcutta, Ohio) and "to tutor all pupils" from children of twenty-three families "commencing the first day of September 1814."[5] Forty-eight students arrived at McGuffey's subscription school. Like other schoolmasters, he taught for ten to fifteen weeks, eleven hours a day, six days a week. The children brought their own books, the Bible being the most usual.

One day the Reverend Thomas Hughes—a Presbyterian minister born in York County, Pennsylvania, a 1797 graduate of Princeton, and the first settled pastor north of the Ohio River—was riding through the wilderness seeking students and funds for his subscription school. While traveling through the countryside he discovered McGuffey, who earnestly desired to further his education. Thus he took McGuffey into his own home at Darlington, some thirty miles away on the Ohio border, and for the next four years McGuffey attended the Old Stone Academy.

While teaching at the University of Virginia later in his life, McGuffey used to talk of the academy and his teacher, Thomas Hughes. It seems that William earned his tuition of three dollars a year by acting as sexton at Hughes' church, and he earned his room and board, seventy-five cents a week, by performing chores at Hughes' home. For two years he lived with the Hugheses, ate bread and milk, worked, and studied on log seats at this primitive frontier school, which prepared youth for both college and the ministry.[6] Supported by the Presbyterian church, the Old Stone Academy began to "Latinize" children for college—particularly those living in Washington County—in 1806. There is no way to know what schoolbooks were used, but those most typically read in frontier academies were Noah Webster's *An American Selection*, Lindley Murray's *English Reader*, Albert Picket's *American School Class Books*, James Ross' *Latin Grammar*, Ruter's *Arithmetic*, Jerediah Morse's *Geography*, and Walker's *Readers*.[7]

William completed his studies with Mr. Hughes, who suggested that he once again return to teaching in order to earn enough money for college. The year was 1820; William was twenty, and Warren, Ohio, was looking for a headmaster to direct a new school. William applied, but he apparently failed to meet the standards set by the two Yale graduates who questioned him, an experience that influenced his decision to enter college without delay no matter what the cost. He immediately enrolled in a class of eighteen at Washington College, a Scotch Presbyterian school incorporated in 1806 at Washington, Pennsylvania. There he lived with the president, the Reverend Andrew Wylie, a thirty-year-old Scotch-Irish Presbyterian minister and an honor graduate of Jefferson College. Wylie took a particular liking to William and seems to have played a major role in shaping McGuffey's later life. For almost six years William alternated between working at home on the farm, teaching school, and attending classes at Washington. When he had no money for books, he copied them in longhand.[8] Poor he might have been, but disciplined determination, hard work, and, perhaps, his mother's desires and Wylie's encouragement drove him on.

During the winter of 1825–26, with still a term remaining to complete his degree in ancient languages and philosophy at Washington College and low in funds, McGuffey opened a private school in Paris, Kentucky. There in the smokehouse of the Reverend John McFarland, pastor of the Paris Presbyterian Church, he held classes. Along with the Bible, the *New England Primer* was his basic text. McGuffey was a strict disciplinarian, and later in his life he expressed regret at this severity and the excessive use of the rod on his pupils.[9] Nevertheless, when the Reverend Robert Hamilton Bishop, a Presbyterian minister, recently elected president of Miami University in Oxford, Ohio, passed through Paris, he was impressed with McGuffey's knowledge of the classical languages and his ability to teach. Bishop had been president of Transylvania·University in Kentucky and pastor of the McCord Presbyterian Church in Lexington. Now as president of Miami University, he was in need of a professor of ancient languages. Bishop offered

McGuffey that position, even before he had completed his degree.

Tradition suggests that McGuffey was enthusiastic but unable to make a decision alone. He returned to his mother and sought her advice. She is said to have encouraged him, but only after he promised to be ordained some day, a promise he fulfilled a few years after she died. He also wrote President Wylie. After William's decision to accept the appointment at Miami, Wylie responded:

> Upon the whole I am inclined to think that you acted wisely in going to Oxford. You had raked up all the information to be found here, and the prospect afforded you there, of being useful, and at the same time preparing yourself for more extended usefulness in the future, while your funds may be accumulating instead of diminishing, I consider singularly felicitous. I did wish you very much to remain and graduate regularly with us, and afterward to settle in some situation within striking distance of me, and in a more civilized land of the world. But I know it must not be according to my mind and I wish you to be where you will be most useful and happy.[10]

In 1826, with an agreement that he would be awarded his A.B. degree from Washington College, William took his young brother Alexander and headed off for Miami.

In looking back over our limited life history of William H. McGuffey, it may be said that four persons were particularly significant in his early life. First and foremost was his mother, whose influence seems beyond measure. He appears to have made her concerns, ambitions, thoughts, and feelings his own. Then there were three Scotch-Irish Presbyterian ministers—William Wick, Thomas Hughes, and Andrew Wylie. McGuffey lived in each of their homes and studied at their sides. Together they not only encouraged his learning and academic pursuits, but they also became role models during his impressionable adolescent years. While living in the parsonages of these teacher-ministers who cared for and encouraged him, with the enthusiasm and support of his mother, McGuffey framed his own understandings and ways of life.

There were obviously other influences as well. The early move from the security of his grandparents' farm and influence, the hardship of the frontier and his mother's desire that he live a different sort of life, his labors at the side of his father on the farm, teaching in his own school at age fourteen, Hughes' providential visit to his home, his failure of the examination for a teaching position in Warren, Ohio, life at Washington College, and Bishop's visit to the Kentucky smokehouse school—each of these events and experiences appears to have been significant in his life. Yet there is still much we do not know. We must ask, for example, why those events and not others were subsequently recorded. Were other educationally significant events and persons left out because of his biographers' ignorance or prejudice? Why is no mention made of the effects of national, political, economic, and social events on his life? Could it be that he was isolated from such happenings? We do not know what books, newspapers, or magazines he read, if any. His known sources of learning are few. Perhaps that is all there were; if so, that too is important to know.

If our emphasis has been on a few particular persons, events, and mostly schooling, it is because that is all the information we can verify. Further, even as we have recorded these influences, we have been forced to make conjectures from corresponding historical records. Nevertheless, we do get the outlines of a picture that is helpful in understanding McGuffey and his work.

Arrival at Miami

Miami University was founded in 1809 (five years after Ohio University) by an act of the Ohio legislature. Nine years later, a small, red house in Oxford, Ohio, was purchased for the president-to-be, and the first college "edifice" was completed—a three-story structure in the middle of twenty acres of recently timbered expanse of maple and beech trees. In the same year a grammar, or preparatory, school was opened. Fifteen years later, the all-Presbyterian board of trustees elected its first president—Robert Bishop, a rugged Scottish preacher educated at Edinburgh University and, for the past twenty years, professor and president of Transylvania College in Kentucky. Soon thereafter, Miami University opened with twenty students ranging from twelve to twenty-three years of age. The following year Bishop described his vision for Miami as the "Yale of the West."[11] By the second year there were sixty-eight students and three members of the faculty: President Bishop, professor of moral philosophy and logic; John Annon of Dickinson College, professor of mathematics, geography, natural philosophy, political economy, and astronomy; and William Sparrow of Trinity College, Dublin, professor of ancient languages. Sparrow soon resigned to become president of Kenyon College, and his successor was William Holmes McGuffey, not yet a college graduate. In the same year, John Witherspoon Scott from the faculty of Washington College became professor of science.[12]

McGuffey was twenty-six years old when he came to Miami on a horse loaded with books on moral philosophy and languages. His ten-year-old brother, Alexander, was with him. When they arrived in Oxford, the McGuffeys found a pioneer village of five hundred residents who had migrated from Scotland, Ireland, England, and the Atlantic states. The town included a number of log and frame houses and one solitary brick home, three taverns, a Presbyterian church, six stores, a harness shop, a livery stable, a tanyard and a stump-dotted campus containing the college "edifice" and president's house. Alexander was enrolled in the grammar school connected with the university, and William began his ten-year career at Miami, a career that was to establish him as the college's most popular teacher and, next to the president, the most influential member of the faculty.[13]

Miami University was exceptional and progressive. Its

students came from all parts of the Miami Valley in Ohio. As early as 1825 it added to its classical course a new English scientific curriculum offering modern languages, political economy, and applied mathematics. By 1829 it had opened a theology department to prepare students for Lane Seminary in Cincinnati and a farmer's college combining a three-year practical program in agriculture with literary and scientific courses. One of this country's earliest observatories was built at Miami in 1836. By that year the faculty had grown to seven and the student body to 234. It was during these years that McGuffey played an influential role.

During his first years at Miami, McGuffey boarded in Oxford. Recollections suggest that McGuffey was of medium stature and compact frame. His forehead was broad, his eyes clear and expressive, and his prominent nose and wide mouth reflected his strong, rugged Scotch pioneer character.[14] On the way to and from the college he passed the home of Charles Spinning, an Oxford merchant. When Spinning's sister Harriet visited from Dayton, she was introduced to McGuffey. She is said to have been a beautiful, intelligent girl, who was four years his younger, modest, and deeply religious.[15] They fell in love, but before McGuffey proposed he wrote Andrew Wylie at Washington College to ask his advice. Wylie replied, "I have no advice for those who contemplate matrimony for they are usually bound to commit it."[16] And so it was that on April 3, 1827, William and Harriet were married at Woodside, the nine-hundred-acre estate of Harriet's father, Judge Isaac Spinning, near Dayton. The Spinning family had migrated from London to New Haven, Connecticut, in 1638 and to Ohio in 1786. Very little is known about Harriet, and almost nothing is ever said about her by William's biographers. From correspondence and from their daughter Henrietta's diary we get the impression that she was a gentle, submissive, warm, conscientious, pious person.[17]

For a short time William and Harriet boarded in the home of John Dollahan—in Oxford's lone brick house—but

Harriet is reported to have been very unhappy with their cramped quarters. In 1828 McGuffey purchased, with help from the estate of Judge Spinning, a four-acre tract of land adjoining the campus. They lived in an existing small frame house for a time, and two of their children were born here. In 1833 McGuffey added a two-story brick house of six rooms valued at eighteen hundred dollars. Soon considered the finest house in town, it was a short walk from the college building where, on the southwest corner of the second floor, McGuffey lectured each day.

While living in Oxford the McGuffeys had four children—Mary Haines in 1830, Henrietta in 1832, William Holmes, Jr., in 1834, and Charles Spinning in 1835. One other child, Edward Mansfield, was to be born in 1838 after McGuffey left Miami. William Holmes, Jr., lived less than a month; Edward Mansfield, about a year; Charles died at the age of sixteen, a year after his mother's death in 1850. The two girls were married—Mary Haines to a physician, Walker Stewart of Dayton, and Henrietta to a Miami University professor, Andrew Hepburn.[18]

Very little is known about William H. McGuffey as a parent. Our only link, Henrietta's diary, lacks any account of the early childhood years. Some insight, however, can be gleaned from some of her later entries. For example, when her father remarried in 1851, shortly after her mother's death, Henrietta wrote: "It seemed to me almost worse than my brother's death, but there was no help for it. We children had only to submit and patiently endure. We had been brought up to such perfect obedience to our parents that nothing but submission did we ever think of."[19] A disciplined life of obedience to parental authority was a fundamental conviction of McGuffey's. Just as important were duty and industry. His own experience had proven their worth.

In a letter to his son Charles, McGuffey wrote:

Let me remind you of the importance of industry and a careful observation of every duty, not ever neglecting your personal habits. Everything depends upon habits framed in youth. This you know, but we are all liable to forget.[20]

Perhaps more important for McGuffey were piety and familial love.

> Remember my dear son to read a portion of the Bible every day and do not forget daily to pray to God to keep you from evil and to prepare you for the duty of life and for the hour of your death. Think of your mother and often ask yourself how *she* would advise and what *she* would think of any course you are about to pursue.[21]

Preacher

Two passions consumed McGuffey—educating the young mind and preaching the gospel. His mother wished him to be a minister, and he wanted to be one himself. Only lack of funds proved an early barrier to that career. Now that he was established as a professor, however, he turned to complete his preparation for the ministry through private study. It is not known with whom he "read" theology. Most likely it was the minister of the Oxford Presbyterian Church to which he belonged. In 1829 he was ordained at Bethel Church in Indian Creek by the Oxford Presbytery.[22] Throughout his life preaching remained one of the McGuffey's greatest loves. (One might say that all his lectures were sermons, his classroom a pulpit.) He not only took his regular turn in preaching at the college chapel, but on other Sundays he traveled throughout the surrounding area, preaching in rural churches. This was a time of bitter sectarian strife and of widespread prejudice against college-educated ministers. Even so, McGuffey triumphed as one of the most popular preachers in Ohio.

McGuffey was primarily known for his sermons on character and behavior. "Without fervor, tenderness, pathos, or passion his religion was morality untouched by emotion."[23] His delivery was quiet and almost conversational in tone.. He abhorred written sermons or speeches, and he was respected for his powerful ability to communicate extemporaneously with all sorts of people. Nevertheless, two handwritten sermons by McGuffey do exist, though there is no record of where or when they were delivered.

These sermons do not provide significant insight into his theology. Neither they nor oral tradition provide any hints whether he was involved in the Old Light–New Light Presbyterian controversy. His sermons appear to have none of the rhetoric or intention of New Light revivalism. Nor is there any record whether he preached on the issue of slavery or the Westminster Confession. While in both existing sermons the Christian faith is presented as rational doctrine, concerned primarily with individual morality and pious behavior, there is scant evidence to help us define his positions.

The New Light–Old Light controversy of 1837–69 had its roots in the early Old-New Side Schism; the issues are unclear, and rhetoric and accusations abound. It is difficult to find anyone who obviously is a member of one party or the other. The best that can be said is that "they looked at things in different lights."

Stated in the extreme, the Old Lights affirmed original sin and the human inability to do good, grace through conversion or regeneration as solely the work of God, justification by faith in Jesus Christ, and eternal election. The New Lights are said to have compromised these Reformation doctrines. They were said to affirm, for example, that man can choose not to sin, that people are not unrighteous by nature but by corrupting influence and bad example, and that education can be beneficial in changing behavior.

There is no evidence that McGuffey was involved in this controversy or that he took a side. In any case it appears as if he was more a product of the Scottish Enlightenment than of these indigenous religious conflicts.

Teacher

Consistent with McGuffey's commitment to the ministry was his interest in moral philosophy. While he had been brought to Miami to teach ancient languages—Latin, Hebrew, and Greek—he was more interested in the courses traditionally taught by the college's president. Longing for an opportunity to teach mental and moral philosophy, he made his wishes known. In fact, he is said to have exerted the threat of resignation to achieve appointment to the president's chair in philosophy.

Reluctantly, President Bishop relinquished his chair in moral philosophy to McGuffey in 1832. Soon thereafter other and more serious tensions between McGuffey and Bishop surfaced. It appears that Bishop was socially progressive and theologically liberal while McGuffey was conservative in both realms. Even McGuffey's dress symbolized his conservatism. Everyone remembered that he wore knee breeches long after they were out of style. Finally succumbing to trousers, he habitually wore a style reminiscent of the past—a glossy, black bombazine coat, a dark clerical tie, and a stovepipe hat—and he carried an ebony cane.[24] The major point of conflict, however, arose over the issue of discipline. Bishop had established the liberal policy of giving students a voice and responsibility in the running of the university. He favored lessening the number of rules and regulations. McGuffey heartily disagreed.[25]

The argument became so serious that in 1836 McGuffey solicited a letter from J. M. Browne, one of his students, in support of his position:

> I do not recall that there ever occurred a single instance of unfaithfulness neither in laxity or rigidity in your department. Some severe cases of discipline have occurred . . . I have seen severity used even to the bringing of tears and to the driving of the individual in fury from the classroom. But I cannot recollect that I have ever seen you even in the strictest moments of severity go further than my judgment approved. I have always been an advocate of strict discipline as you and the other instructors in this institution have long known.[26]

In the same letter, Mr. Browne sided with McGuffey, asserting that discipline at Miami is "too lax." He praised McGuffey's competence and faithfulness as a teacher and was appalled by the rumor that poor discipline influenced McGuffey to resign.

On the whole, the faculty at Miami sided with their president. Professor Scott in particular objected to McGuffey's position, calling him a hypocrite who, while calling for strict discipline at faculty meetings, has

> on the other hand to the students appeared magnanimous. I have myself observed a very great difference between the tone assumed by McGuffey respecting a young man in secret faculty session and when the young man was present before us. In the one case he has been harsh, laconic and denunciatory in the extreme—in the other smooth as oil.[27]

In spite of his apparent disagreements with the faculty, McGuffey seems to have been genuinely liked by students, at least in nostalgic retrospect. Thomas Millikin (1838) expressed the feelings of many when he wrote that McGuffey was "a model teacher studiously dignified and polite, elegant and accomplished in social life, critical and exact in knowledge, with unusual capacity to impart knowledge to others."[28]

Judge Caldwell (1827) called him a "conscientious, laborious and successful teacher" to whose scholarly qualities can be added "the charm of unassuming practical religion."[29] Governor Anderson (1833), being more objective in his evaluation of this "young underdeveloped scholar," commented that McGuffey was "doubtless as good a classic scholar as Washington College could at this date graduate . . . and by the standards of Western institutions he was superabundantly able to teach any class of persons Latin and Greek."[30]

"The impression made by Professor McGuffey in the classroom was that he was a born educator. . . . He inspired us with the love of knowledge and taught us how to think," commented the Reverend B. W. Childlaw (1833). It is further reported that McGuffey was a master at illustrating abstract propositions with concrete examples. His mind was clear, orderly, and exact, his language ready and precise. "He was rich in pungent phrase and anecdote, apt in citation from history, literature and life, skillful in analogy."[31]

"He made himself, like Socrates, the intellectual midwife of this students, stimulating and clarifying their ideas with compelling interrogation." It is said that he was usually genial with students, but it was a sort of "calculated, conscious geniality."[32] Very slight provocation would make him "austere, harsh and stern."[33] Thornton writes that he was often cruel (or was it a misunderstood sense of humor?). He records a conversation in which a student commented, "I am very fond of your lectures, Dr. McGuffey, but I find them difficult and make little headway." "Yes, sir," answered McGuffey, "I have noticed that your appetite for moral philosophy is much better than your digestion." Of another student, he is said to have remarked, "His head is like a gourd full of gnats; plenty of ideas, but badly arranged."[34]

An example of the teaching style McGuffey affirmed and defended can be found in his essay "Conversations in a School Room."[35] This essay is important for a number of reasons. First, it gives some insight into McGuffey's thoughts on discipline; second, it provides us with clues to his understanding of teaching. There is some evidence that McGuffey was dissatisfied with teaching as he knew it. He is recorded to have said that many schools were "slaughter houses of minds." Perhaps that explains his early desire to provide new resources for teachers and children. In any case, in spite of a strenuous schedule as full-time college professor (teaching eight to ten hours a day) and a part-time Presbyterian preacher, he found time to experiment with the ways children learn to read. Previously he is said to have published in London "A Treatise on Methods of Reading."[36] Now, as tradition has it, he sought an opportunity to test some of his theories. Gathering a number of neighborhood youngsters on his porch, he attempted to establish which stories were readable and most appealing to children of particular ages. In the process, he became convinced that it was not necessary to learn to spell before learning to read. It was better, he found, to begin with whole words in sentences, providing they were related to pictures. Further, it was best to learn to read by reading aloud. Obviously, younger children needed shorter sentences and briefer lessons than older children, but all children learned moral virtues best (the primary aim for learning to read) through real-life human interest stories that were read aloud and memorized.[37]

As early as 1830, McGuffey had begun to compile the contents for a series of readers by arranging neighborhood children into age groups and trying out a variety of lessons on them. Apparently he wrote, collected, and tested numerous stories, making notes on his observations from day to day, changing and adopting them until he found the "right ones." In this manner, McGuffey gradually gathered a collection of his own writings, clippings from periodicals, lessons from other schoolbooks, and selections from standard literary works (including the Bible) for possible use in schoolbook readers. By 1833 it is recorded that he had completed a first reader and had accumulated a great deal of material for later use.[38]

Reading was not McGuffey's only interest. Rhetoric, or the activity of elocution, held a central place in the curriculum of most colleges during the era because the ability to speak well was useful in all professions—ministry, law, teaching, and politics. Since no one else at Miami was prepared to teach elocution, McGuffey took it upon himself to meet with interested students each morning before breakfast.

McGuffey was known to possess the abilities both to speak in public and to teach others to do so. He put his charges through a demanding pace, requiring each in turn to declaim before his critical ear. Next came speaking in the college chapel and then, perhaps, preaching in one of the rural congregations near the university. The latter was important because, as Professor McGuffey told his students, "There you can prove your elocution and learn to put your thoughts into simple sentences that the illiterate can understand."[39]

His interest in rhetoric made him a natural faculty sponsor for the debating society. Most often he was appointed critic. In 1829 he participated in one well-publicized debate with two Universalists. Depending on his Greek New Testament and Pauline doctrine, he won a smashing victory.[40] A few years later he wrote his son Charles:

> I am pleased that you take interest in the debating society—it is an excellent way to improve the members in both your thinking and speaking. But it requires more preparation than is usually given it.
>
> I think the best way is to reflect a good deal on both sides of every question and if time can be opened, to write down your thoughts on both sides, but *never* to take the paper into the society, nor even try to remember the words you have written.

In the same letter he mentions possible topics for debate: "Which is of greater influence on society, woman or man?" He comments: "In favor of women one might say that our first mother gave character to the whole race." Another subject suggested was "May a man tell a lie to save his life?" In the negative, McGuffey writes, "You may urge that it is better to lose the whole world than the soul."[41]

McGuffey emphasized the spoken word throughout his life. Even in his Readers he directed that children should read the lessons aloud to reinforce their message, and he encouraged memorization. We are told that he prepared to speak by pacing the floor of his room arranging and memorizing his thoughts aloud. After one delivery, being asked for a copy, he replied, "Gentlemen, I have no copy and never had. I could hardly make one. Please excuse me."[42]

Writer

In spite of his busy schedule as teacher, elocutionist, debate coach, preacher, lecturer, parent, compiler of schoolbooks, and ex-officio librarian at the college, he made time to become the founder of the college's literary society, the Eradelphians, and its journal, *Literary Focus*, and even to write a number of short stories. Two things seem clear. McGuffey brought to every task an abundant amount of energy and a corresponding desire to persuade the world of his religious and moral convictions.

During 1834 he anonymously published a number of articles in the *Western Monthly Magazine*. Beginning in 1830 as the *Illinois Monthly*, the *Western Monthly Magazine* ran from 1833 to 1837. Published by Corey and Fairbanks in Cincinnati, the center of western culture, its editor, James Hall—a pioneer lawyer and judge—was committed to the new literature of the West. With a circulation of three thousand, its regular contributors included William Gallagher, Hannah Gould, E. W. Mansfield, and Harriet Beecher.[43] As was common practice each contribution was published anonymously. Nevertheless, there is a record of four pieces by McGuffey in one issue which we know of only because of the editor's autographed bound edition of the *Western Monthly Magazine* (1834) in which McGuffey is identified as their author.[44] Two are narrative stories: "James Kirkwood: A True Narrative," and "Seth Bushnell: A Yankee Trick." The other two are essays: one on education and the other, a theological discussion entitled "Reverie." The latter essay is representative of his mode of thinking and style of communication. His two sermons, his other writings, and the text for an unpublished book, "Mental Philosophy," written late in his career, read very much like this essay. It is in stark contrast to the text in his *Eclectic First* and *Second Readers* but not atypical of the material he chose to include in the *Eclectic Third* and *Fourth*.

McGuffey liked to think of himself as a philosopher, and he took great pride in his philosophical utterances. "Reverie" begins with a long, tedious argument about the relationships of effects and their causes. He makes the point that something that does not tend directly or indirectly to the accomplishment of the end in view cannot be attributed to the efficient cause. That is, we attribute the defects of a painting not to the design of the artist but to his lack of skill or the imperfection of his materials. He then argues:

> By the criteria of passivity, the coherence of activity with passive organization, and the limited faculties and specific application of finite minds, we ascertain the universe—the world of matter, mind and relations—to be an effect. But from its stupendous magnitude, its irresistible energies, and its unequivocal evidences of design, we ascribe to its cause the attribute of infinite power controlled and directed by infinite wisdom. This would seem to be the lowest character of the Creator deducible from his works, even in ruins.

McGuffey continues by affirming that since the natural attributes of the Creator are infinite power and intelligence, the primitive character of his creation must logically express those attributes. Such a Creator acts according to and in pursuit of a definite plan. Everything was *originally* consistent and harmonious with such a design.

McGuffey then suggests a number of reasons why suffering and evil cannot proceed from God as their efficient cause. Suffering and evil are disorders and defects; such are not possible in the perfect system that God establishes.

"Evil is a matter of fact." But McGuffey is sure that our Creator God is not its cause. Admitting that no one can finally establish evil's origin, he speculates that it originated through the voluntary agency of a moral subject. God created a perfect world in which "the morning stars sang together and all the sons of God shouted for joy." In the beginning all things were good. Matter accurately obeyed the laws that were impressed upon it, and mind voluntarily retained its proper relationships to the great center of the moral system; but this latter did not continue.

We can still witness God's perfect creation in nature in the instincts of animals. We should therefore affirm that God created the world "to promote the glory of the Creator by such means and such alone as should be indispensable to the happiness of the creature." All life leads directly to the moral end for which it was designed. "All else must be pronounced to be the work of the destroyer." [46]

McGuffey's theology was not original. In all his known theological utterances, he emphasized the role of reason, used nature as the basis for his convictions, and focused on the moral life. Yet he doesn't clearly fit into any "school" of the period.

From the evidence available, it seems that McGuffey's mind was little changed during his years at Miami. Rather it was in these years that he sought ways to express his convictions and apply them to the education of children. I have found no evidence that any experience after 1836 significantly affected his life or thought. The radical experiences of his childhood and youth appear to have molded his thoughts and feelings. Nothing caused him to waver; with a single-minded determination and commitment, he spent his life striving to pass on his convictions to the next generation.

Educational Reformer

McGuffey's early years were his formative years; his ten years at Miami were his productive years. He proved himself in the classroom, pulpit, and lecture platform; with the written and spoken word; as linguist, classicist, and philosopher. Like the three pastor-teachers who nurtured him, he envisioned religion and education as interrelated and essential to a healthy society.

Often, we are told, when the Ohio legislature was in session he traveled to Columbus in support of the common school cause. Early in his career at Miami he joined the physician, Daniel Drake; the lawyer-philanthropist, Edward Deering; the seminary professor, Calvin Stowe; the first state commissioner of education, Samuel Lewis; the principal of a female seminary in Cincinnati, Albert Picket; and the schoolbook author, John Ray, in a campaign to secure better-trained teachers for the public schools through the formation of teachers' training institutes and professional associations.[46]

In this regard, McGuffey was one of the early and most active members of the Western Literary Institute, or, as it was originally named, the College of Teachers. Early in the nineteenth century the teachers of Cincinnati had organized for mutual aid and improvement. On June 20, 1831, Albert Picket proposed a plan for organizing in one body the teachers in all public and private schools and the friends of education. Their first meeting was on October 3, 1832. The Western Literary Institue was one of the most important early attempts to organize the teaching profession in the United States. Its aim was simply to promote the "sacred institution of education." To achieve this objective the association affirmed the need to educate the general population about education and to elevate the character of teachers.

Many committees of the Western Literary Institute claimed McGuffey as a member. For one term he served as president. Numerous actions are specifically attributed to him; two motions bear his name. One motion was in support of female education:

1st. Resolved, That while the American nation is distinguished for a high regard for the female character, and for the attention given to female Education, still there is much which needs to be attempted in order to secure a proper education to those who necessarily must have the most influence in forming the mind and heart of the coming generation.

2d. Resolved, That the interests of female Education demand the endowment of female Seminaries for the education of female Teachers; and, also, for those who are not directly designed for that office.

3d. Resolved, That the evanescent and fluctuating character of female schools, are serious obstacles to all attempts at a thorough and systematic course of female education.

4th. Resolved, That in order to secure stability to female institutions, a certain combination of measures is necessary, not demanded in institutions for the other sex—these are: 1st. Buildings appropriate, and trustees provided by public or private influence. 2d. That the Principal Teachers of such institutions should be females. 3d. That Associate Principals be employed in each institution, instead of giving it to the sole supervision of a single individual. These three measures combined are deemed indispensable in order to secure that degree of permanency and system to female institutions that now appertain to those for the other sex.[47]

A second motion dealt with the proper relationship between common and sabbath schools. It reads: "Sunday School instruction is so analogous to a right system of instruction in common schools that peculiar reason ought to exist to authorize school officers to refuse the Sunday School the use of public school houses." The members of the institute agreed, affirming that when "Sunday Schools are properly conducted they are a most valuable auxiliary to the common schools."[48] Interestingly, we can find no evidence that McGuffey was in any way related to the Sunday school movement, which during this period was so significant on the frontier.[49] It appears that McGuffey considered the public schools the proper place for religious and moral instruction, or at least that is where he chose to exert his influence.

In the field of education, McGuffey is credited with having written what might be described as a progressive, enlightened report entitled "On Examinations," found later in this volume. He is also credited with two lengthy responses in favor of motions before the institute. The first response defended a report on the importance of the classics. "We naturally and correctly take interest in everything ancient, especially if connected with the efforts of human life and genius," McGuffey contended.[50] In responding to a report concerning methods for teaching English composition, he supported those newer methods that encouraged and employed original composition. From these two comments it appears that McGuffey supported traditional ends but progressive means.

Eighteen hundred thirty-five marked the fifth annual convention of the Western Literary Institute and the College of Professional Teachers. At this occasion, McGuffey gave one of his rare recorded addresses, "Duties of Parents and Teachers." In September of the previous year McGuffey published an article entitled "General Education" in the *Western Monthly Magazine*, providing us with further insight into his understanding of education.

Schoolbook Compiler

In a letter to Winthrop B. Smith, of the Cincinnati-based publishing firm of Truman and Smith, dated September 17, 1834, William H. McGuffey wrote:

> It pleases me to notify you that I have today completed the manuscript of the first reader, according to the agreement made in my home in Oxford on 28 April 1833. I intend to have the manuscript for the second reader plus that of the speller in your hands for publication within the first month of the forthcoming year.
>
> I am also delighted to inform you that the trunk of books containing leading editions of similar children's textbooks of the East which you were kind enough to send have promise to be of the greatest assistance. I pray that our venture proves to be satisfying not only to myself but to yourself also.
>
> I remain, Sir,
Yours with respect
William Homes McGuffey[51]

Bookmaking and publishing, a long-time established enterprise in Boston, Philadelphia, and New York, had spread west with the migration of some Eastern printers who chose to publish under the motto "Western books for Western people."

In 1835 Truman and Smith was a small, embryonic publishing firm on the second floor of 150 Main Street. Its small list of books included mostly reprints of standard works likely to sell in the Midwest: *The Picture Primer, The*

Picture Reader, Smith's Practical and Mental Arithmetic, and *Smith's Practical Grammar*. The year before, they had published their first copyrighted book, *The Child's Bible*, and others soon followed: Mason's *Sacred Harp* and Joseph Ray's *Eclectic Arithmetic*, the first in a very successful series of arithmetic texts.[52] Sales were good. Expansion seemed wise.

Of the two partners, the young entrepreneur Winthrop B. Smith from Stamford, Connecticut, was convinced that the firm's economic future was in schoolbook publishing. He, therefore, set out to find an author to compile a complete series of school readers adapted to the values, beliefs, and ways of those who had migrated and immigrated to the Middle Border.[53] Anthologies seemed best; they were both practical and popular. By the gathering of selected pieces from numerous sources, eclectic readers could provide the best literature available.

For his compiler, Smith sought an eminent educator and established writer. One of the initial persons he is said to have considered was Catherine Beecher, a well-known new arrival from Connecticut, the eldest daughter of the Reverend Dr. Lyman Beecher, president since 1832 of Lane Seminary. Before coming to Cincinnati, Miss Beecher had established the Female Institute for Girls in Hartford, Connecticut. She had already written the arithmetic and other texts used in that school and, with her sister Harriet Beecher Stowe, had published *Primary Geography for Children*. Only recently she had opened the new, but already respected, Western Female Institute.

Mr. Smith reportedly asked Miss Beecher to compile a series, but she declined. Her time was already committed to the higher education of women. McGuffey's biographers—Minnich, Vail, and Ruggles—suggest that she recommended McGuffey. While there is no firsthand evidence to support that contention, there is no reason to doubt it either. We know that the McGuffeys, Beechers, and Stowes were longtime friends. For years they had worked together in the Western Literary Institute. McGuffey was also well known in the Cincinnati area and indeed was more than likely a familiar name to the publisher. In any case, Truman and Smith offered McGuffey the opportunity to compile a series of four graded readers, and he agreed to do so.

Henry Vail claims that McGuffey prepared the first two Readers of his series by gathering a small group of children at his Oxford home. Arranging them in age groups, he is said to have sought to understand their interests, reading ability, and comprehension. In this manner we are told he gathered appropriate material for the books.[54] Smith chose the word "eclectic" to describe the nature of these schoolbooks. The title was appropriate. McGuffey compiled most of his Readers by borrowing from other texts and literary sources. As such sources were few, it was difficult to avoid material that overlapped with the books of other publishers. In 1830, Richardson, Hart and Hobrook published *Worcester's Primer* and *First Book for Reading*. Four years later they published a *Third* and *Fourth Reader*. It appears that McGuffey used some of the same lessons contained in the Worcester Readers. In 1838, shortly after McGuffey's *Eclectic Third Reader* came off the press, the publishers of the Worcester Readers brought suit against Truman and Smith and W. H. McGuffey (now president of Cincinnati University), charging McGuffey's texts with "over-imitation" and the violation of copyright, especially in the *Eclectic Second* and *Third Readers*.

Most books published at this time borrowed from one another. Charges of plagiarism could easily have been hurled at any number of authors and textbooks. Edward O. Mansfield, a prominent Ohio educator, perceived this situation and defended McGuffey in the *Cincinnati Daily Gazette*. He stated the publisher's charges bore no weight since materials for most textbooks were "acquired by the free exercise of a pair of scissors and the entry of the title page in the District Clerk's office." He further noted that the copyright law applied only to original works.[55] Catherine Beecher also wrote in defense of McGuffey. Her letter reprinted in the *Common School Advocate*, a publication of Truman and Smith, explained that it was the McGuffey Readers' popularity and financial success alone that had precipitated the erroneous charges.[56] A few months later the suit was dropped. McGuffey reworked his original text by making a few slight changes, such as changing a title from "Cat and Ball" to "Puss and Kittens" and the content of a lesson entitled "About the Sun" to one "About the Moon." Along with the addition of one lesson, "The Story of Jonah," Truman and Smith published the revised editions in 1838. A long publisher's preface to this revised edition included the following:

By reference to our title page, it will be perceived that we present our patrons with an improved edition of the Eclectic Reader.

The cause of this revision, not being generally understood, we will briefly state it.

Certain compilers of school books, in New England, feeling themselves aggrieved that our books contained a portion of matter similar to their own; matter which was considered common property, have instituted legal proceedings against us for this correspondence with a view to their immediate suppression.

We have no objections to meet them on their own grounds. But for both, and for all, there is another tribunal than the law. The public never chooses school books to please a compiler. That public, then, is the tribunal to which appeals of this character ought to be made; and as the correspondence between ours, and other publications are few, and immaterial; we had hoped that the compilations of the East and the West would have been thus left to stand or fall upon their own merits.

But this course, recommended alike by a just self-respect, and a proper regard for the public wish, has not been pursued. These compilers have resorted to the law, and an effort is now making, not only to force their own books in the Western market, but to wrest from Western talent, and Western enterprise, the legitimate fruits of a preserving [*sic*] toil.

They mistake the spirit of the West, however, who think they can thus force it into any channel. It has the intelligence and chooses well; and having thus chosen, no combination can move it from its purpose. We have then no cause for anxiety or alarm; and so far as our interests are concerned, we feel secure against any attack.

But to place ourselves entirely in the right, and to remove every cause for cavil or complaint, we have expunged everything claimed as original, and substituted other matter, which, both for its fitness and variety, will add to the value of the Eclectic Readers. We never intended to wrong any compiler, here or elsewhere; nor do we feel that we have done so. But now we *know* that we have not; and as in the effort to accomplish this object we have *improved* our books; neither the public nor ourselves can regret the cause which has produced it.

We offered the former edition under no peculiar advantages. All that we promised was fidelity to our trust, and an honest endeavor to meet the wants of the West. It was a new enterprize, and in undertaking it, we had no patronage, no combination, to foster it or support it. The books had to undergo the severest scrutiny, and we had to compete with old and strong claims. But they *succeeded* and we are rewarded.

There were no further entanglements, but other competitors continued from time to time to accuse McGuffey of unfairly using material from their books. Competition and the success of McGuffey's Readers seem to be partially responsible for these accusations.

All through this period, Truman and Smith differed on the significance of their venture in schoolbook publishing, and so, a few years later (1841), the partnership dissolved. Minnich explains that Smith brought the disagreement to a head by stacking in two piles the books published by the firm. In one he put all the firm's cash and all their books except the few schoolbooks Smith had commissioned. These made a smaller pile. Truman is said to have chosen the larger pile and the cash, leaving Smith the sole owner of McGuffey's Readers and a few other texts.[57]

From 1841 to 1852 Smith continued to publish the McGuffey Readers. In 1841 he signed a contract with William's younger brother Alexander for a rhetorical guide, published in 1844 as the *Eclectic Fifth Reader*.

Truman and Smith were only the first of seven publishers

during the Readers' almost one hundred years of publication. Each publishing house produced numerous revised editions. Eighteen fifty-two marked the year that Smith admitted his wife's brothers, Edmund and Daniel Sargent, as partners, changing the name of the firm to W. B. Smith and Company. They published a newly revised edition of the *Eclectic Readers* in 1857. That was the same year that Alexander compiled a sixth Reader and McGuffey's name was made the headline of the series, though by that time William H. McGuffey had little to say about their contents.[58] Indeed McGuffey's continuing relationship to the Readers was peripheral from the beginning. In his original contract he accepted a royalty of 10 percent on all sales until the royalties reached a thousand dollars. He contracted to receive additional funds for revisions. When revisions were made, however, McGuffey was never asked to contribute.

From 1863 to 1868 the publishing firm for McGuffey's Readers was Sargent, Wilson, and Hinkle—Wilson being the major continuing editor-revisor. It was he who had directed the first major revision of 1857. The name of the firm was changed once again in 1868 to Wilson, Hinkle and Company. Then in 1877 the publishing rights to the Readers were bought by Van Antwerp Bragg and Company. Two years later, under the editorship of Henry Vail, another complete and radically revised edition of the series appeared in a new uniform binding. This 1879 edition became the most popular of all. 1890 marked the year the American Book Company became the sole owners of the copyright.

While there were four Readers in the original set, few schools needed more than the first two. Only in the most populous centers was the entire series used. The Fourth Reader was written for the highest levels of ability in the elementary schools, and much of the literature in it was of secondary school difficulty.

Twice as many lessons are found in the Second Reader as in the first. Each story is accompanied, as in the First Reader, by vocabulary-spelling words, but in addition, there is a series of questions to aid the teacher in reviewing the meaning of the story. For example:

Questions: 1. What is the subject of this lesson? 2. What is it to swear? 3. Is it a foolish habit? 4. Is it polite to swear? 5. Is it very wicked? 6. What is said about profane swearers in the Bible?

The advice to teachers in the front of the Second Reader suggests that the children begin by reading each story aloud; they are then to retell the story in their own words; finally they are asked the questions at the end of the story. All of this is to check whether the story has been understood and its "lesson" learned.

The Third Reader most likely was read by children in the equivalent of our fifth and sixth grades. Its sixty-seven lessons are much longer than those of the Second Reader, the vocabulary more difficult. Unlike the First and Second Readers, the Third contains a collection of essays or excerpts by identified authors. Many were written by eighteenth-century American Congregational (Puritan) clergymen, such as Lyman Abbott, Samuel Worchester, Charles Hawes, Samuel Nott, Timothy Flint, John Cotton, and McGuffey's friend Henry Ward Beecher. Some were by educators, such as S. G. Goodrich, Harriet Beecher, Lydia Huntley Sigourney, and the sixteenth-century Protestant educator Johannes Sturm. A large number of other authors were also clerics or religious writers from the United States and England, such as Unitarian William Channing; Baptists Jonathan Maxey, Robert Hall, and James Addison; Presbyterians John McDuffie and Ebenezer Erskine; Methodist Charles Everett; Episcopalians Stephen Tyng and James Porteous; and the Protestant dissenter Francis Mason. Six lessons are taken directly from the Bible: two from Psalms, two from Isaiah, one from the Book of Solomon, and one from the Gospel of Matthew, namely, the Sermon on the Mount. Eighteen lessons are poems. More than half the authors are American. Lessons most often deal with contemporary problems, such as temperance or the public schools. Some lessons were written by authors living in the Cincinnati area, such as Drake and Beecher. Numerous English authors are used—for example, Francis Bacon, George Washington Doane, John Milton, Lord Byron, William Shakespeare, and Sir Walter Scott. Among the authors there are also numerous political figures, such as Noah Webster, Thomas Jefferson, Jean Jacques Rousseau, and William Blackwood, and reformers, such as Archibald Grimke.

In the schools of the period, public speaking was an important part of the curriculum. Elocution was an important aspect of every public occasion. A rhetorical guide was therefore included in the Readers. Along with vocabulary words and questions typical of the other period readers, there were rules for reading that accompany each lesson. For example, the first lesson begins with these words:

1. Hold your book up well and do not bend forward. 2. Speak each word distinctly and be careful to pronounce correctly. 3. Endeavor to understand what you read.

Directions such as the following are found throughout the book: "Pieces of a melancholy nature should be read in a soft style. Imagine yourself in the author's place and you will read as you should."

The questions that close each lesson tend to be informational and primarily rhetorical. For example, following a story entitled "The Consequences of Idleness," the first question is, "What is the story about?" The obvious answer is idleness. The next two questions are "What did George Jones think about most?" and "Was this wise?" The story made very clear that George thought the young could spend their time in any way they please and that this is not wise. Another question reads, "What must we do to escape the disgrace which fell upon George?" The obvious answer is be not idle. Then the lesson asks, "Do you think there is any idleness in heaven?" Of course the proper response is no, for idleness is sinful and ruinous. The final question reads: "If we wish to secure an interest in heaven, what must we guard against?" The answer once again is idleness. And thus the questions reinforce the moral of the story.

The Fourth Reader was, generally speaking, the last Reader most children during the mid-nineteenth century ever used. Before a child completed its 324 pages of 130 lessons, he or she would have completed elementary school. Emphasizing that it contained extracts in prose and poetry from the best of American and English writers, the Fourth Reader offered the student fifty-one poems and seventy-nine pieces of prose, sixteen taken directly from the Bible. There were also pieces by Shakespeare, Milton, Bacon, Doane, Byron, and Washington Irving as well as by friends of McGuffey, such as Catherine Beecher. Like the Third Reader, the Fourth had rules for reading, directions for avoiding common errors in pronunciation, and questions for discussion. The print was small, and there were no accompanying pictures.

In the Fourth Reader, the teacher is directed to have students read the story aloud and retell it in their own words. Next they are to write the story as they remember it without the aid of a dictionary or grammar. Once the pupils can read, retell, and write the story, they are to turn to the questions to make sure they understood its meaning and have learned its intended lesson.

While we have no primary sources on the intentions or means by which William H. McGuffey compiled his Readers, some insights can be gleaned from the prefatory material published in his first editions.

For example, in the preface to the Fourth Reader are some comments on apparent criticism of the pictures and questions in the First and Second Readers:

> Much, has at times been said and written against the use of cuts, or *Pictures* as employed in books for children, such as the First and Second Eclectic Readers. But the author cannot bring himself to believe, that those who employ this

declamation, can mean any thing more than that pictures are liable to *abuse*, in the business of instruction. And what is there that is not liable to abuse?

There is no person but the veriest smatterer [*sic*] in the business of education, who does not see at once, that visible delineations are indispensable in every grade of education, from the primer to the Principia. What are maps in Geography,. or cuts in Natural History, or diagrams in Geometry, but visible delineations on precisely the same *principle* with pictures and cuts in elementary books for children?

On the subject of *Questions* appended to the lessons, there is, and can be, but one opinion amongst the intelligent in community. Where answers are furnished to every question the memory alone will be cultivated. But no teacher *can* give instruction without *asking questions.*

The compiler will rejoice to know, that those who use his books, ask more intelligent questions, and in much greater numbers, than are to be found in the pages before them. This is the very design of that part of his labors. His wish is, to incite the teacher to the interrogative method *orally*, and then he cares not whether he asks a single question that is printed in the book. Still, he believes that some teachers may be found, who are not too wise to be *assisted* in this manner; and who may not only need, but feel that they need such suggestions as are furnished in the questions.

A final comment in the preface to the Fourth Reader provides insight into the compilation of all four Readers:

> In conclusion, the author begs leave to state, that the whole series of "Eclectic Readers" is his own. In the preparation of the rules, etc., for the present volume he has had the assistance of a very distinguished Teacher, whose judgment and zeal in promoting the cause of education have often been commended by the American people. In the arrangement of the series generally, he is indebted to many of his friends for valuable suggestions, and he takes this opportunity of tendering them his thanks for the lively interest they have manifested for the success of his undertaking.
>
> From no source has the author drawn more copiously, in his selections, than from the sacred Scriptures. For this, he certainly apprehends no censure. In a Christian country, that man is to be pitied, who at this day, can honestly object to imbuing the minds of youth with the language and spirit of the Word of God.

The student of the Bible will, it is believed, be pleased to find a specimen of the elegant labors of Bishop Jebb, and some specimens of sacred poetry as arranged by Dr. Coit, in which the exact words of our authorized translation are preserved, while the poetic order of the original is happily restored.

McGuffey's intentions are clarified again in the preface to the *Eclectic Third Reader:*

To those into whose hands this book may fall, who may not have seen the numbers intended to precede it, the Compiler begs leave to state, that he has aimed to combine *simplicity* with *sense; elegance* with *simplicity*, and PIETY, with both; so far as these qualities *can* be combined with that which is transferable to a printed page.

For the copious extracts made from the Sacred Scriptures, he makes no apology. Indeed, upon a review of the work, he is not sure but an apology may be due for his not having still more liberally transferred to his pages the chaste simplicity, the thrilling pathos, the living descriptions, and the over-whelming sublimity of the sacred writings.

The time has gone by, when any sensible man will be found to object to the Bible as a school book, in a Christian country; unless it be on purely *sectarian* principles, which should never find a place in systems of general education. Much less then, can any reasonable objection be made to the introduction of such extracts from the Bible as do not involve any of the questions in debate among the various denominations of evangelical Christians.

The Bible is the only book in the world treating of ethics and religion, which is not sectarian. Every sect claims *that* book as authority for its peculiar views.

The rapid sale of seven editions of the First and Second Readers, within a few months, gives the author additional confidence in both his principles and his plan of arrangement. With these few prefatory remarks this work is respectfully submitted to a liberal public.

In the preface to the Third Reader we also find a series of suggestions from McGuffey to teachers. They begin by recommending that the pupil be required to master everything in the book as he proceeds from lesson to lesson. We read:

The Definitions ought to be made out by the exercise of the pupil's own judgment (aided by the instructor,) from the sense which the *connection requires:* for, to seek out and memorize definitions from a dictionary, or defining vocabulary, is injurious rather than beneficial. It is a mere exercise of memory, and nothing else.

McGuffey continues:

The plan of teaching the pupil to *spell,* in conjunction with the exercises in reading, will, it is believed, be found eminently beneficial in fixing in the memory the *orthographical form of words,* not only as they appear in the columns of a spelling-book or dictionary, but in all the variety of their different numbers, oblique cases, degrees of comparison, moods, tenses,—while the exercise of *defining* produces a similar effect in regard to the *meaning* of the terms employed; since the learner is required to find out the meaning of each term defined, from the *connection,* without having recourse to an expositor.

It is the *connection alone,* that can convey to the mind the true meaning of words. No two words in any language are exactly alike in signification. How then can definition, *merely,* be made to convey their import?

And finally he comments:

The questions appended to each lesson are, as in the preceding volume, designed to *suggest* rather than to *direct* the interrogative method of *oral* instruction. The teacher will frequently find questions, the answers to which are not contained in the antecedent lesson, but only suggested by it. This is calculated to awaken inquiry, on the part of the pupil, and to lay the instructor under a kind of obligation to read the lesson over carefully before he attempts to hear it recited by the learner—a plan which the author cannot too earnestly recommend in regard to *every possible kind* of teaching.

To explain the difference between the four Readers, the preface to the Fourth Reader stated:

The main difference between this and the "Third Eclectic Reader" is, that the rules are more specific—the exemplifications more numerous—the list of errors more extended—and the interrogations more copious, embracing a wider range, and requiring a more vigorous exercise of thought, in order to provide intelligent, and intelligible answers.

The selections for the present volume are of a higher grade of literary and intellectual excellence. The mind of a pupil is presumed to have improved, and expanded, as he advanced through the preceding numbers of the "Series," or its equivalent in other books. In this therefore, he is to expect, that higher claims will be made upon his powers of thought; and larger contributions be levied upon what he may, (or ought to) have learned from other sources.

All he knows, and, not unfrequently, more than he knows, will be put in requisition by the questions appended to the lessons here presented. It is deliberately intended to lead the mind of the pupil, as often as practicable, beyond the pages of the book in his hands. Let him not think this unfair. Nor will he, for a moment, entertain such an opinion, if his mind is sufficiently active and vigorous to take delight in new efforts, and fresh acquisitions.

We often seem to make *discoveries;* and certainly do make advances in knowledge, by being somewhat importunately interrogated upon topics, with which our previous acquaintance was neither accurate nor extensive. It rouses the mind to successful effort, and often strikes out new and brilliant views of a familiar subject. And who, that has made one acquisition of this kind, does not desire frequently to repeat the experiment?

It continues:

But this book is designed for other purposes than merely to teach the pupil to read. The selections have been made with a constant reference to the improvement of the *mind* as well as to the cultivation of the voice. Many of the lessons require thought, in order to be appreciated, and before they can be comprehended. Some of these require an extensive range of reading and deep reflection, to enable the reader fully to understand the allusions, to enter into the spirit, and to realize the excellence of the extracts.

Let the *teacher* then *study* the lessons as well as the pupils. Let him require, that the substance of what has been read be continuously narrated by the pupil *without* recurrence to the book. Let him direct that this be *written down* without the aid of a dictionary or grammar, and with no other appliances at hand than pen, ink, and paper. Let each pupil be so situated that he can derive no assistance from his fellow pupil; and then let the narratives, both oral and written, be the subject of severe but candid criticism by the teacher and the other pupils, as to the style, pronunciation, grammar and penmanship.

Let the teacher sometimes read aloud a lesson to his class, having previously removed every means of taking *notes* while he reads—and then let him require each pupil within a given, but sufficient time, to render in writing and from recollection, an abstract of what he has read.

This exercise improves the attention, practises the pen, gives fluency of expression, and a readiness of employing the ideas gained in reading, as capital of our own; and will be found highly interesting to the pupils and highly improving in a greater variety of ways than many other highly approved methods of recitation.

Shortly after their publication, McGuffey's Readers received acclaim. J. M. Stowe, a classical and elementary school teacher from Lexington, Kentucky, wrote a testimonial letter to the publisher on December 14, 1836.

The books are such as to impart clear and well defined ideas to the minds of pupils. The proper gradation is observed in the selection and arrangement of lessons—keeping pace with the increasing ability on the part of the reader to overcome new difficulties, a deficiency of most of the juvenal books hitherto published. A fine moral effort is made in these lessons which should be ranked among the prominent merits of these books.[59]

An advertisement published in the Fourth Reader included a review signed by E. D. Mansfield, inspector of common schools and professor of constitutional law in Cincinnati College; C. E. Stowe, professor in Lane Seminary; John W. Hopkins, professor in Woodward College; Lyman Harding, Asa Drury, and Daniel Drake, professors in Cincinnati College; Baxter Dickinson and Thomas J. Biggs, professors in Lane Seminary; Hiram P. Randall, J. G. Evans, Cyrus Davenport, E. Dolph, and Darius Davenport, principals of common schools; William

H. M'Cracken, trustee of common schools; M. R. Deming, principal of classical school; John Burtt, pastor of Fourth Presbyterian Church and former editor of the *Standard;* and S. N. Manning, principal of Beech-Grove Academy. Commenting on the First Reader, they wrote:

It is, without doubt, practically as well as philosophically correct, to employ those words, as far as it could well be done, which enable the child to use the sounds he has learned, instead of puzzling him, prematurely, by a promiscuous use of *all* the sounds of each vowel. We think that a child, using this Reader, will be able with comparative ease, to form letters into words, and acquire a knowledge of their sound, in their various combinations.

The second difficulty is removed, as far perhaps as it can be, by selecting such words as the children themselves employ in forming their own sentences. The words and sentences are short and simple.

The third difficulty is remedied in various ways. Pictures are employed to excite curiosity, and the lessons are fashioned to illustrate the pictures connected with them. When the child is thus incited to study out the meaning, he will find the sentences very easy,—usually, containing one simple idea, and that idea such as will delight him. The scenes, the sports, the ideas, the language, are all familiar to him, without being chargeable with silliness or vulgarity. In a word, we feel warranted to express great approbation of the skillful adaptation of this work to the *real and peculiar* difficulties, which a child encounters when first beginning to read.

On the Second Reader, they commented:

Having by this time acquired the ability of reading, it is proper that the pupils should use it for purposes of *instruction.* We observe that, in the Second Reader, much important information is interwoven with the texture of sprightly stories, which a child can hardly fail to remember. To facilitate this effect, questions are appended as *hints* to the teacher, when he examines his scholars concerning the *meaning* of what they have read. Upon the whole, we think the preparation here, for readers in the second stage of progress, is as happy as that which the previous work presents for beginners.

Concerning the Third, they concluded:

> When children enter upon this book, they are supposed to be pretty good readers, so far as *ready pronunciation,* and comprehension of words, are concerned. . . . In the Second Reader, the child was taught to understand the meaning of sentences; in the Third, he is led on to the definition of *words,* and suitable questions are prepared for this purpose. Vulgar habits of pronunciation are noticed and corrected; and every means is seized upon, which may excite attention and thought; promote deliberation and accuracy; and make scholars *intelligent* and *intelligible* readers.
>
> But one step more remains for Mr. McGuffey, which is, to give a sufficient number of reading lessons for practice in the various *styles* of prose and verse; to introduce the pupils to the highest kinds of composition; and to exercise them in the principles of intonation. It is presumed that the "Eclectic Fourth Reader," will do this.
>
> We have examined these books with a view to their adaptation to the peculiar wants of schools, and we think them fitted, in a very eminent degree, to the *real* wants of scholars in the different stages of their progress in reading.

In the preface to the Third Reader, Catherine Beecher is quoted as saying:

> I have, by request, examined the "Eclectic Readers," and am decidedly of opinion that they unite more advantages than *any other* works of the kind, which, after extensive opportunities for examination, have yet come to my knowledge. The advantages consist in a combination of excellences that are scattered in many works, but united so far as I know, only in this.

A number of reviews of the first editions of McGuffey's Readers appeared shortly after they were published. In the *Cincinnati Journal and Luminary* we read:

> We are sincerely pleased with this series. The works evidence much care. The selections are very simple, very entertaining, and of unimpeachable morality.
>
> We think no school can use them without some of the following effects, viz.—great facility on the part of the teacher—great ease in understanding them, and (if the

questions be adopted) great progress in learning to think of what they read.

They are got up in a very superior style; the paper is good and the type clear. We see no *Eastern books* with which the Eclectic Series would not compete *to great advantage.*[60]

The *American Presbyterian*, published in Nashville, Tennessee, commented:

Until very recently, it must be admitted that the First Books for children have been miserably defective in this one point—they have been utterly unsuited to the age and capacity of the learner.

We are therefore inclined to support and value every attempt to remedy the evil. We have looked over two of these Books, and though we should not pretend to decide upon the whole course upon so slight an examination, yet, we have from these two, formed a favorable opinion of the "Eclectic Series," and think them as well adapted as any thing we have seen to the capacity of the learners for whom they are designed. The Readers are progressive, useful in their subject matter, and written so that at each stage of its progress the young mind can grasp the whole *meaning* without too great an effort to understand the *words.*[61]

This high praise appeared in the *Baptist Journal of the Valley of the Mississippi:*

These are new works. They combine, in a high degree, the prime excellencies which should characterise Reading Books for children and youth in our schools. They are filled with pieces easy to be understood and interesting to the young mind. This is necessary, to fix the attention. They furnish a rich storehouse of interesting facts on various subjects and sound moral principles, which being treasured up in the youthful mind, will prove of great value in after life.

The simple easy style of the pieces, together with the interesting matter they contain, will be highly favorable to the formation, in the pupil, of an easy natural manner of Reading—an acquisition, which is made with difficulty when such books as Murray's Reader, for instance, are used. We commend the Eclectic Readers to the notice of Teachers.[62]

Today, original copies of the first Truman and Smith editions of the McGuffey Readers can be found at the McGuffey Museum, Miami University, Oxford, Ohio; the Henry Ford McGuffey Museum, Dearborne, Michigan; Ohio State Collection, Columbus, Ohio; and the Maude Blair Collection, Detroit, Michigan. Significant collections of all the editions of the Readers can be found in the New York Public Library, the Cincinnati Public Library, and the American Book Company.

After Miami

While Cincinnati was the economic, social, and intellectual center of the Midwest, it lacked a first-rate university. Daniel Drake, a man of vision, sought to reorganize Cincinnati College for that end. At the time McGuffey believed that Miami was passing through dark days. Disturbed by the discipline question and in disagreement with its president, he was enticed by Drake to come to Cincinnati. After ten fruitful years of teaching at Miami, McGuffey resigned on August 26, 1836, to become president of the reorganized Cincinnati College.[63] Drake himself was dean of the medical school, and Edward Mansfield was dean of the school of law. Unfortunately, a year later a financial panic of national proportions destroyed the university's future, and in 1839 the school closed its doors.

Drake and his friends saw to it that McGuffey did not suffer from this economic failure. Ohio University, the oldest educational institution in the state, was in need of a president. During its thirty-five-year history, the school had never attracted more than 90 students. In 1839 McGuffey assumed the presidency, and in a year the enrollment rose to 196 students. But from the beginning he was unpopular with the townspeople. Apparently the campus had become a community cow pasture, but McGuffey found this unforgivable and put a fence around the campus. The townspeople revolted; he was burned in effigy and pelted with mud balls. The people petitioned the state legislature to cut the college's appropriations. Further difficulties ensued at the college. Because of his strict disciplinary stance, in 1841 only one of sixteen seniors received a diploma. Taxes for the university were increasingly difficult to collect from farmers who saw little use for higher education. Sick at heart and distressed over economic affairs, he resigned in 1843 after four unhappy years.[6]

McGuffey moved with his family to Cincinnati and lived with his brother Alexander. For a short time he was professor of languages at Woodward College, which was a good classical high school. It was during this time that Alexander compiled the *Eclectic Fifth Reader*. McGuffey's position at Woodward was only temporary, and in 1845 he was called to be professor of philosophy at the University of Virginia. The faculty vote, it appears, was split on his appointment; for while McGuffey was not an abolitionist, his emancipationist tendencies were not appreciated by some.[65] Nevertheless, he taught at Virginia for twenty-eight years. During that time he was offered the presidency of Miami in 1847 and again in 1868, but each time he chose to remain at Virginia. His wife died in 1850, and he remarried the following year. He and his new wife had one child, who died at the age of four. On May 4, 1873, at the age of seventy-three McGuffey died; he was buried at Charlottesville, Virginia. Just before his death he completed the text for a book on mental philosophy or psychology. It was never published, but the manuscript can be found in the McGuffey Museum at Miami University.

It would be not an overstatement to say that the pinnacle of McGuffey's career was during the ten years he taught at Miami University and that as far as it can be determined the mind and spirit of McGuffey were most fully expressed through the compilation of his Readers.

Notes

1. Harvey C. Minnich, *William Holmes McGuffey and His Readers* (New York: American Book Company, 1936), pp. 10-11.
2. William B. Sweet, *Presbyterian Religion on the American Frontier*

(New York: Harper, 1936), pp. 526, 527.

3. William E. Smith, "William Holmes McGuffey—Mid American," *Bulletin of Historical Society of Ohio*, January, 1959, p. 41.

4. William H. Venable, *Beginnings of Literary Culture in the Ohio Valley* (Cincinnati: Robert Clark & Co., 1891), p. 195.

5. Contract between McGuffey and West Union, September 1, 1814, McGuffey Collection, Miami University, Oxford, Ohio.

6. W. M. Thornton, "The Life and Service of William Holmes McGuffey," *The Alumni Bulletin of the University of Virginia*, July, 1917, p. 237.

7. Venable, *Literary Culture*, p. 193.

8. A Hebrew grammar in McGuffey's handwriting is on display at Washington and Jefferson College.

9. Robert Sanders, *Presbyterians in Paris and Bourbon County, Kentucky, 1786-1861* (Louisville: Dunne Press, 1961), pp. 46-47, 35, 49-50.

10. Wylie to McGuffey, February 11, 1826, McGuffey Collection, Miami University.

11. Alfred Upham, *Old Miami: The Yale of the Early West* (Hamilton, Ohio: Witaker-Mohler, 1947), p. 20.

12. Walter Havighurst, *The Miami Years* (New York: Putnam's, 1971), p. 85.

    After two years in the preparatory school, Alexander McGuffey went to Washington University. There he received his degree at sixteen and was soon teaching English at Woodward College in Cincinnati. Six years later he passed the bar and began the practice of law. It was Alexander who compiled the Fifth and Sixth McGuffey Readers.

13. Thornton, "Life and Service of McGuffey," p. 237. See also Havighurst, *Miami Years*, p. 83.

14. Vail, *History of the McGuffey Readers*, p. 29.

15. Ruggles, *Story of the McGuffeys*, p. 69.

16. Wylie to McGuffey, January 31, 1827.

17. Diary of Henrietta McGuffey Hepburn, McGuffey Collection, Miami University.

18. Smith, "William Holmes McGuffey," n.p.

19. Diary of Henrietta McGuffey Hepburn.

20. McGuffey to his son Charles, September 10, 1851.

21. McGuffey to his son Charles, October 3, 1850.

22. Ruggles, *Story of the McGuffeys*, p. 70, sets the date as 1833. Vail sets the date at March 29, 1829, in *History of the McGuffey Readers*, p. 25. Neither date can be substantiated by any records of the presbytery. The earlier date seems more likely.

23. Sam Greer, *The Miami Student* (Oxford, Ohio, May 1905), n.p.

24. Thornton, "Life and Service of McGuffey," p. 240.

25. Havighurst, *Miami Years*, p. 60.

26. Browne to McGuffey, August, 26, 1836.

27. James Rodabough, "A History of Miami University to 1845" (M.A. thesis, Miami University, 1936), p. 129.

28. Thomas Millikin, "Reminiscences of Dr. W. H. McGuffey," *The Miami Journal*, March, 1888, p. 123.

29. J. M. Caldwell, "Reminiscences of McGuffey," p. 116.
30. Charles Anderson, "Reminiscences of McGuffey," p. 125.
31. B. W. Childlaw, "Reminiscences of McGuffey," p. 116.
32. Thornton, "Life and Service of McGuffey," pp. 238, 242.
33. Anderson, "Reminiscences of McGuffey," p. 126.
34. Thornton, "Life and Service of McGuffey," p. 242.
35. W. H. McGuffey, "Conversation in a Schoolroom," *Monthly Chronicle of Interesting and Useful Knowledge*, March, 1839, p. 147.
36. Minnich, *McGuffey and His Readers*, p. 32. Regretfully, this manuscript appears to be no longer in existence.
37. Vail, *History of the McGuffey Readers*, p. 32.
38. *Ibid.*, pp. 34, 35.
39. W. E. Smith, *About the McGuffeys* (Oxford: Cullan Publishing Co., 1963), pp. 7, 8.
40. Anderson, "Reminiscences of McGuffey," p. 123.
41. McGuffey to his son Charles, March 15, 1851.
42. Sanders, *Presbyterians in Paris and Bourbon County*, p. 49.
43. R. L. Rusk, *The Literature of the Middle West Frontier* (New York: Appleton, 1925), p. 170.
44. "Contributions to the *Western Monthly Magazine*" (1834), mimeographed, McGuffey Museum, Miami University, n.p.
45. W. H. McGuffey, "Reverie," *Western Monthly Magazine*, May, 1838.
46. Benjamin L. Crawford, *William Holmes McGuffey: Schoolmaster to a Nation* (Delaware, Ohio: Carnegie Church Press, 1963), p. 74.
47. "Transactions of Eighth Annual Meeting of the Western Literary Institute, Oct. 1838" (Cincinnati, Ohio: Executive Committee, 1839), pp. 16, 23.
48. *Ibid.*, p. 24.
49. See Robert Lynn and Elliott Wright, *The Big Little School* (New York: Harper, 1971).
50. William Holmes McGuffey, 'Remarks on Motion to Adopt Report of Methods of Teaching English Composition,' "Transactions of Fifth Annual Meeting of the Western Literary Institute, Oct. 1835" (Cincinnati, Ohio: Executive Committee, 1836), p. 230.
51. McGuffey to Smith. The date of the contract differs. Henry Vail, in *A History of the McGuffey Readers*, p. 33, suggests October 12, 1835. This original letter substantiates an early date.
52. Nietz, *Old Textbooks*, p. 72.
53. Vail, *History of the McGuffey Readers*, p. 28.
54. *Ibid.*, p. 32.
55. *Cincinnati Daily Gazette*, February 28, 1839, p. 2.
56. Catherine Beecher, "Literary Piracy and Moral Assassination," *Common School Advocate*, 1839, pp. 194-96.
57. Vail, *History of the McGuffey Readers*, p. 41.
58. *Ibid.*, p. 52.
59. J. M. Stowe to Truman and Smith, December 14, 1836, McGuffey Collection, Miami University.
60. *Cincinnati Journal and Luminary*, August 11, 1837, p. 14.
61. *American Presbyterian*, September 20, 1837, p. 8.
62. *Baptist Journal of the Valley of the Mississippi*, October 15, 1837, p. 3.

63. Harvey Minnich, *William Holmes McGuffey and the Peerless Pioneer McGuffey Readers* (Oxford, Ohio: Miami University, 1928), p. 25.
64. *Ibid.*, pp. 26, 28.
65. *Ibid.*, p. 29.

CHAPTER III

America's Most Popular Schoolbooks

A great many generalizations have been made about the content of the McGuffey Readers. Still, few people have any clear idea of the teachings William Holmes McGuffey intended to transmit to the children in the common schools of mid-nineteenth–century America. This chapter summarizes the findings of a complete content analysis of the first editions of the four *Eclectic Readers* under the categories of world view and value system.

A world view and a value system are universal aspects of culture. In his book *Understanding Religious Man*, Frederick Streng wrote:

> Man's conduct is regulated not only by "instinct" or physical limitations; his activity is also conditioned by "values," patterns of judgment and expression which indicate one's place in an *order*. Man, further, seeks for the meaning of his experience; that is, he places his hopes, frustrations, sense, observations, likes and dislikes into a world view, an outlook on life. [1]

A world view is a person's systematic and comprehensive concept of his or her world. A world view provides a meaningful framework for a discussion of the perspective out of which persons answer questions about life. In McGuffey's Readers, the natural categories for description are God, the natural world, and humankind.

A value system is a concept that makes possible a systematic description of the behavioral guides that undergird persons' lives. Two sorts of values can be described, namely, terminal values, those concerned with life goals, and instrumental values, those concerned with guides for conduct. A terminal value is understood as a person's conviction that a particular end state of existence (salvation, for example) is preferable and worth striving for. An instrumental value is understood as a person's conviction that a particular mode of conduct (honesty, for example) is personally and socially preferable. Such a system explains the ranking of particular values along a continuum of importance so that when two or more values are in conflict a choice can be made.

World View

Most commentaries on McGuffey's Readers discuss the moral and spiritual values they extoll, but eschew the world view that undergirds them. To ignore the theological world view in the first editions of McGuffey's Readers, however, is to miss their significance and misunderstand their content.

Even a cursory reading of these early schoolbooks reveals their dominant concern for the character and nature of God and his relationships with persons and the world. Correspondingly, statements about the natural world focus upon the role nature plays in helping us to understand God and his ways. Consistently, the Readers affirm the ultimate insignificance of this world and the greater importance of the world we enter after death. The most prevalent material on human nature deals with rewards and punishments granted to persons in the next life for living or not living according to God's will.

God

It is difficult to conceive of William H. McGuffey compiling schoolbooks for children in which God is not central. He learned to read the Bible at his mother's knee and continued to study its contents from his earliest years at Wick's subscription school, through his preparation for the Christian ministry, until his last days as a Sunday school teacher at the University of Virginia. The three educators most influential in his life were Scotch-Irish Presbyterian ministers. He lived in their homes, studied in their schools, and worshiped in their churches. Piety and learning were never separated in either his life or work. Indeed, the mind and spirit of McGuffey cannot be understood apart from his understanding of God. Neither can his Readers.[2]

From the First to the Fourth Reader, belief in the God of the Old and New Testaments is assumed. When not mentioned directly, God is implied: "You cannot steal the smallest pin . . . without being seen by that eye which never sleeps."[3] More typically, however, lessons make direct references to the Almighty: "God makes the little lambs bring forth wool, that we may have clothes to keep us warm. . . . O, let me not speak bad words; for if I do, God will not love me. . . . All that live get life from God. . . . The humble child went to God in penitence and in prayer. . . . All who take care of you and help you were sent by God. He sent his Son to show you his will, and to die for your sake."[4]

Nevertheless, while God-consciousness is taken for granted, McGuffey's Readers assume that all true knowledge of God is dependent upon "God's book," the Bible. God sent us his Word for our eternal benefit. Within the pages of the Bible, God reveals himself, the mystery of creation, the nature of human life and death, and all that he requires us to know, believe, and do. Most important, in the Bible we learn that God uniquely reveals himself in the life, death, and resurrection of Jesus Christ, without whom our lives have no meaning or purpose.[5]

No book is more important than the Bible. Indeed, McGuffey's interest in teaching children to read is directly related to his conviction that knowing the contents of the Scriptures is of ultimate significance. Thus, he not only includes many lessons about the Bible, but he also uses much material taken directly from the Old and New Testaments.

When we investigate the content of McGuffey's Readers, three dominant images of God emerge. God is creator, preserver, and governor. Just as the Old Testament opens with God creating and revealing himself through his creation, so the Readers treat nature as "the glorious mirror of God":

> The Spacious firmament on high
> With all the blue ethereal sky,
> And spangled heavens, a shining frame,
> Their great Original proclaim.
> The unwearied sun, from day to day,
> Does his Creator's power display;
> And publishes to every land
> The work of an Almighty hand.[6]

God, we are told, made the sun and the moon, the plants and the trees, the animals, and at the very end, God made humans in his image, living souls.[7] All things owe their existence to him. God is not simply *a* creator, he is *the* creator of heaven and earth, the ultimate source of the universe. To prove this point, McGuffey uses a lesson from nature in which George Washington discovers his name written in cabbage plants. He runs to his father with excitement, having guessed that his father must have planted the seeds in this manner. George's father proudly comments that his son has guessed rightly, but he explains that he grew the cabbage plants to teach his son an important lesson:

"George, you were correct. The plants could not have grown in that pattern by chance. Someone had a *design* and the fact that they grew as they did is evidence that some 'agent or being' was involved. Now here is the point," explains George's father. "Look at the beautiful, orderly, purposeful world. Isn't it true therefore that there must have been a designer—someone who formed things for a purpose—for some end?"[8]

God is the creator, and his creation enables us to understand him. In proportion as we investigate the secrets of the natural world, we are able to understand the nature of God. Consider the rainbow. As a phenomenon of nature, it is a glorious sight. But it is more than a beautiful picture God has given us to enjoy. God has made it a sign of his providence.[9]

God, the creator, is the preserver of life and of our lives. God is not simply a "first mover" nor has the world been left entirely to us. God continues to act in his world, to govern and to preserve his creation. God creates, and God preserves. "God gives us food to eat and clothes to make us warm."[10] We owe everything, "good health . . . home . . . parents . . . friends . . . books . . . enjoyments" to God.[11] Nothing we are and nothing we possess can be understood apart from his actions. It is even reasonable to believe that "the Lord has been very good to us to place us in a part of the earth where we have such pleasant seasons."[12]

God is the great provider:

John, you must always bear in mind, that it is God who made you, and who gave you all that you have and all that you hope for. He gave you life and food and a home to live in.

All who take care of you and keep you were sent by God. He sent his Son to show you his will and to die for your sake.

He gave you his word, to let you know what he had done for you and what he bids you to do.

He is always present and acting among us.

Who is it that gives us food to eat and clothes to make us warm?

It is God, my child; he makes the sun to shine and sends the rain upon the earth, that we may have food.

God makes the little lambs bring forth wool, that we may have clothes to keep us warm.[13]

God not only provides us with all our necessities; his providence works in and through the lives of men and women. For example, "Luther was raised up by Providence to be the author of one of the greatest and most important revolutions recorded in history."[14]

In a lesson describing a sea voyage in which the author is tossed overboard, we read:

I felt as if God had flung me at once from the heart of joy, delight and happiness, into the uttermost abyss of moral misery and despair. Yes! I felt that the almighty God had done this,—that there was an act, a fearful act of Providence, and miserable worm that I was, I thought the act was cruel. . . . I gnashed my teeth and cursed myself,—and with bitter tears and yells, blasphemed the name of God.

It is true, my friend that I did so. God forgave that wickedness. The being, whom I then cursed, was, in his tender mercy, not unmindful of me—of me, a poor, blind, miserable, mistaken worm.

As the story continues, we find the author floating aimlessly and helplessly at sea. As he feels himself dying, a calm comes over him, and he prays for the forgiveness of his sins. When he wakes, he is safe on board a ship. The story ends: "The hand of God was there . . . the merciful God took pity on me."[15]

The providence of God is demonstrated in every aspect of life. God is guiding and directing, not only individual lives, but also social history. The story of "Noah and the Deluge" is a personification of the Readers' conviction that God acts in history for his own good purposes. In the account of the death of Absalom, Ahimaaz is called before the king and says, "All is well. . . . Blessed be the Lord thy God, which hath delivered up the men that lifted up their hand against my lord the king."[16]

Especially has God, the provider, been active in the

establishment of the United States. "After our fathers had passed through a great many trials . . . the Lord blessed their labors and smiled upon them."[17] God was, likewise, providentially involved in the War of Independence.

> The consequence of American independence will soon reach to the extremities of the world. . . . Here in America stands the asylum for the distressed and persecuted of all nations. . . . Its torrents will swell into the heavens, rising above every tempest; and the pillar of divine glory, descending from God, will rest forever on the summit.[18]

No theme is more prevalent than that of God's providence. Neither the world nor our lives can be understood without God. One lesson asks, "Suppose matter to be eternal or without beginning, what is still the evidence of a designing God?"[19] The answer: to have eternal matter there must be "behind it" or "beyond it," an invisible eternal mind in which everything else participates. God who is that intelligent mind, without beginning or end, is also like a human parent; God loves, feels, watches, listens, and ministers to our every need. We are totally dependent upon him. "All that live get life from God."[20]

> On the whole subordinate domain of nature and of providence, he bows a pitying regard on the very humblest of his children and sends his reviving spirit into every head and cheers by his presence every home, and provides for the wants of every family, and watches every sick bed, and listens to the complaints of every sufferer; and while by his wondrous mind, the weight of unusual government is borne, oh! is it not more wondrous and more excellent still, that he feels for every sorrow, and has an ear open to every prayer.[21]

God, the creator and provider, is omnipresent, omnipotent, omniscient.

> God sees and knows all things, for God is everywhere. He sees me when I rise from my bed, when I go out to walk and play. And when I lie down to sleep at night, he keeps me from harm.

Though I do not see the wind, yet it blows round me on all sides: so God is with me at all times, and yet I see him not.[22]

God is the eye that never sleeps; he never leaves us out of his sight. God is hiding behind every corner and under every bed. It is impossible to get away from him. Nothing escapes his eyes:

> O Lord, thou hast searched me and known me. Thou knowest my down sitting and mine up rising. Thou understandest my thought afar off.
> Thou compassest my path and my lying down, and art acquainted with all my ways. For there is not a word in my tongue, but lo, O Lord thou knowest it altogether. Thou hast beset me behind and before and laid thine hands upon me. . . .
> Whither shall I go from thy spirit? or whither shall I flee from thy presence? If I ascend up into heaven, thou art there: If I make my bed in hell, behold, thou art there. If I take the wings of the morning and dwell in the uttermost parts of the sea: Even there shall thy hand lead me, and thy right hand shall hold me.[23]

Thus God the creator and preserver is also the governor, the Lord, the heavenly monarch, who, seeing all and knowing all and having all power, clearly inspires gratitude and obedience. The road to eternal happiness is this:

> Let a sense of our happy situation awaken in us the warmest sensations of gratitude to the supreme Being, let us consider him as author of all our blessings, acknowledging him as our beneficent parent, protector and friend.[24]

God is good to us. In gratitude, we ought to obey him. Correspondingly, "If we do his will, he will love us and will be our God." In any case, "In him [we] live and move. . . . When he says the word, we all must die."[25]

God also wishes to help us. We "should ask for those things which he can give and which no one else can give," knowing that if we ask, he can keep us from both sin and harm.[26]

God governs all of life. He judges, rewards, and punishes.

Those who are judged most severely are those who "return no thanks to God, neither do they fear or obey him."[27]

Clearly, McGuffey's Readers present us with a God-conscious, God-centered world, a world in which God reveals himself through nature, but most significantly through the Bible, as creator, preserver, and governor of all life. Our proper response is to fear, obey, and be grateful to him for all his goodness to us.

The Natural World

From the perspective of McGuffey's Readers, every object in the natural world, like every phase of experience, can be understood properly only in relation to God. That is, everything in creation is grounded in and expressive of God's purposes. We, therefore, live most meaningfully in harmony with nature. Our ideal environment is not what we have created but what God has created. We are called to be stewards of God's creation. While acknowledging that we all benefit from God's creation, the lessons in McGuffey's Readers impress upon us the point that we are not to misuse nature for our benefit. Respect, not control, is our proper relationship to the natural world.

A person may speak of "my" garden or property, but everyone knows that these are only entrusted to our care. God created them, and they are his. He has given the care of his creation to his creatures and will one day require an account of our faithfulness.

God designed nature for our benefit, both for our physical needs and spiritual training, but we are never to forget that the natural world belongs to God. We depart from a steward's life close to nature at our peril. Further, the design of the world is evidence of God's faultless planning. Nature, therefore, can be studied to reveal the character and glory of God.

The natural world, in McGuffey's Readers, is—like God—orderly, beautiful, and good. First, we live in an orderly, cause-and-effect world. If you pull a dog's tail, he will bite you. If you give a cat some milk, she will love you.[28] The moral lessons from nature should be clear. An evil act results in punishment while a good act receives a reward. Those who disobey their parents suffer. Honesty pays, lying does not; goodness benefits, evil does not.

In the moral world of McGuffey's Readers, evil never pays. If for some unknown reason we are not punished in this world, we will be punished in the next. Most often, however, an evil act reaps an evil result here and now. Take, for example, the story of "The Boys Who Did Mischief for Fun," which appears in the Second Reader. Their evil act is to tie grass across a well-used path and hide to watch a series of people trip as they pass by. Eventually a man comes running by, falls, and is seriously injured. As if justice is being acted out before our eyes, we are told that this man was on his way to get a doctor for the mischievous boys' sick father. The story never states whether their father dies, but it does comment that the boys learned their lesson and never misbehaved again.

We reap what we sow. We get what we deserve. "You cannot receive affection unless you also give it. You cannot find others to love you, unless you also love them." "If you are not loved, it is good evidence that you do not deserve to be loved."[29]

Further, the danger in performing one evil act is the natural tendency to progressively perform more and more such acts, until there is no hope. One lie, one act of stealing, will lead to eventual destruction. This understanding is made particularly clear in lessons about drinking alcoholic beverages. "No little boy or girl should ever drink rum or whisky, unless they want to become drunkards."[30]

Second, the natural world is beautiful. This orderly cause-and-effect world is filled with beauty. Every aspect of nature represents "proud monuments of God." Indeed, "the groves were God's first temples." We are therefore encouraged to retire from activity and be in solitude with the natural world:

> Be it ours to meditate
> In these calm shades, Thy milder majesty,
> And to the beautiful order of Thy works,
> Learn to conform the order of our lives.[31]

Any ugliness or disorder we perceive in the world results from a lack of understanding. God has created a beautiful world, and every leaf and flower reveal to us his love and goodness.

Third, the natural world is good. Why? Because God is working out his purposes in and through it. Nothing is without a purpose or use. Everything is "clothed by the hand of Providence exactly in conformity with their wants and the nature of things."[32]

Consider the coral insects:

> These are among the wonders of God's mighty hand; such are among the means which He uses to forward His ends of benevolence. Yet man, vain man, pretends to look down on the myriads of beings equally insignificant in appearance, because he has not yet discovered the great offices which they hold, the duties which they fulfil, in the great order of nature.

Nothing is made in vain; everything in creation has a purpose, namely, the "welfare and happiness of man."[33] In "The Thunder Storm," two boys discuss lightning. One questions lightning's value because it destroys lives and sometimes burns buildings. His friend corrects him, defending lightning as a blessing from God. We need to understand, he points out, that lightning burns up the poisonous vapors that rise from the earth, thereby purifying the air we breathe. "All the works of God are founded in wisdom and are intended for some benevolent purpose."[34]

God's creation is good, and while evil is real, God is not its cause. God created a perfect world in which "the morning stars sang together and all the sons of God shouted for joy." In the beginning, all things were good, wrote McGuffey. All creation obeyed the laws of God. We can still witness God's perfect creation in nature. Evil enters the world by the voluntary actions of men, but nature is still able "to promote the glory of the Creator" and provide us with knowledge of how we should live. This message is consistent with the Readers' lessons.[35]

Man may act against God's will, but finally, God's creation and his creatures will be brought to the goal originally intended for them, namely, eternal life or salvation. Continuously, therefore, the Readers affirm that this life is not our home. We are living in "a state of probation or trial and discipline intended to prepare us for another. . . . We will enter upon active service in another world."[36]

The purpose of this life is preparation for "another world."

> By minds drawn thitherward, and closely linked
> In the celestial union; 'tis in this
> Sweet element alone, that we can live
> To any purpose.[37]

No matter what happens to us, we need not fear, for

> in this world our friends and our parents die; they go away from us, and we see them no more. And here we all suffer much pain and trouble.
> But there is a land where there is no affliction. There no one is sick or dies. Our best friend—the Lord Jesus—who died for us on the cross, lives there. He is the Lord and ruler of that happy land. He will send his holy angels to bring all those who love him, to live with him for ever.[38]

Immortality is assumed. We will be rewarded or punished in the next life according to our behavior on earth. Each person faces a day of judgment, when God decides who will enter heaven and who will be cast into hell—both of which are envisioned as real places. When we die, our bodies are buried and turn to dust, "but our spirits will not be there. Far away beyond the cloudless skies, and blazing suns, and twinkling stars, it will have gone to judgment." And what then will happen?

> You will see the throne of God. . . . You will see God, the Savior, seated upon that majestic throne, and Angels in

numbers more than can be counted, will fill the universe with their glittering wings and their rapturous songs.[39]

At our day of judgment, all our works and actions will be examined.

And do you think they [the heavenly host] will wish to have a liar enter heaven and be associated with them? No! They will turn with disgust. The Savior will look upon you in his displeasure. Conscience will rend your soul. And you must hear the awful sentence, "Depart from me, into everlasting fire, prepared for the devil and his angels."[40]

Significantly, the future is not only for individuals but for all of God's creation.

We did not in our darkest hour, believe that God had brought our fathers to this Godly home to lay the foundation of religious liberty, and wrought such wonders in the preservation and raised their descendants to such heights of civil and religious liberty, only to reverse the analogy of his providence and abandon his work.[41]

Thus, in spite of numerous selections on nature and the natural world, the dominant thrust of the lessons is directed toward another world. The Bible is said to teach us "the vanity of the present world and the glory reserved in a future state for the pious servants of God."[42] It is for this other, more important world that we are to live in this world.

Humankind

"O what a miracle to man is man!" exclaims McGuffey's Fourth Reader.[43] God created persons and set before them the ways of life and death. He gave them language that separates them from the rest of the natural world.

Do you know why you are better than puss? Puss can play as well as you, and can run as fast as you, and faster too; and she can climb trees better; and she can catch mice which you cannot do.

But can she talk? No! Can she read? No! Then that is the reason why you are better than puss—because you can talk and read.[44]

He also gave persons ability to reason. "The chief difference between man and the other animals consists in this, that the former has reason, whereas the latter have only instinct."[45]

The animal kingdom lives in unity with God and his purposes, but it does so without choice. Persons are different. They have choice. And their glory is that they can praise God and live as he wills them to live.

On this much there is general agreement throughout McGuffey's Readers. But beyond this, the Readers' understanding of humankind is unclear. Two fundamentally different traditions are affirmed. According to one minor tradition, each of us is a being in process, who, beginning life in a proper relationship to God, has the possibility of continuing to grow in that relationship. God the Creator has made us capable of endless improvement.

> God has given you minds which are capable of indefinite improvement; he has placed you in circumstances peculiarly favorable for making such improvements; and to inspire you with diligence in mounting up the shining course before you, he points you to the prospect of an endless existence beyond the grave.[46]

Most important is proper education, for persons must "cultivate their minds, improve their talents, and acquire the knowledge necessary to enable them to act with honor and usefulness."[47]

In contrast to this optimistic attitude toward human nature, the major tradition in McGuffey's Readers states that we are all born in a state of sin. According to this view, we are destined for eternal damnation.

> Alas! what have I gained by my laborious labors, but a humbling conviction of my weakness and ignorance? How little has man at his very best estate, of which to boast! What

folly in him to glory in his contracted power or to value himself upon his imperfect acquisitions.[48]

But God has not abandoned us in our misery. There is hope for those who repent of their sins and turn to him in faith.

> There is more joy over the one child that was found than over the ninety and nine that went not astray. Likewise there is joy in the presence of the angels of God, over one sinner that repenteth. . . . The mother cannot feel for her child that is lost, as God feels for the unhappy wanderers in the paths of sin.[49]

We deserve damnation, but God in his mercy has sought to save us. "The Savior has died and suffered for us. He is able and willing to save all who seek the forgiveness of God through him." Therefore, "Let the wicked forsake his way, and the unrighteous man his thoughts, and let him return to the Lord and he will have mercy upon him; and to our God and he will abundantly pardon."[50]

Consistent with this understanding of human nature, good works are evidence of faith. In a lesson praising the Puritans of New England, we are reminded that

> God was their king; and they regarded him as truly and literally so, as if he had dwelt in a visible place in the midst of their state. They were his devoted, humble subjects; they undertook nothing which they did not beg him to prosper: they accomplished nothing without rendering him the praise; they suffered nothing without carrying up their sorrows to his throne; they ate nothing which they did not implore him to bless.
> Their piety was sincere; it had proof of a good tree, in bearing good fruit; it produced and sustained a strict morality.[51]

McGuffey's Readers place great importance on maintaining this strict morality. But the issue of sin and the moral life is very unclear. Two quite different understandings of sin exist side by side. They can best be described in terms of the Presbyterian Old and New Light controversy discussed in the preceding chapter. Like the two understandings of human nature, both of these positions are found in McGuffey's Readers. The Readers have no clear position on human nature or sin. Nevertheless, what we do find are very clear positions on what sins should be avoided or what behaviors a child of God will follow. For example, two of the worst sins are idleness and lying. Faithful children are industrious and tell the truth.

> Remember, child, remember,
> That God is good and true;
> That he wishes us to be
> Like him in all we do.
>
> Remember that he hates
> A falsehood or a lie—
> Remember, he will punish
> The wicked by-and-bye.[52]

"Every child who would be a Christian and have a home in heaven must guard against this sin [idleness]," for if "you are not diligent in the improvement of your time, it is one of the surest evidences that your heart is not right with God."[53]

Love of money is another serious sin.

> Of all God made upright and in their nostrils breathed a living soul, most fallen, most prone, most earthy, most debased is the miser who lives for money. He is also the greatest fool for those in material abundance often die of utter spiritual want.

The avaricious love of money, when operating even upon honest pursuits, is the root of all evil. It is better, then, to beg than to tamper with conscience, sin against God, and lose your soul. Cheating and lying may indeed bring about wealth and distinction, but we should be careful not to envy those with such riches; for riches acquired in such ways ultimately bring the curse of God. And remember, there is an hour coming "when one whisper of an approving mind, one smile of an approving God, will be accounted of more value than the wealth of a thousand worlds like this."[55]

It is wiser, therefore, to be content with life as it is, to be industrious, but not to strive after wealth or abundance. Giving in to present pleasures is clearly a mistake. George Jones is an example of a person who never learned that lesson. Instead of studying diligently at school, he chooses to play. He pays a severe price for being unwilling to accept delayed gratification. In the end, playful George becomes a poor wanderer, without money or friends. Charles Bullard is wiser. Charles thinks of the future. He is praised and rewarded for putting study ahead of play and recess; as a result, when he grows up, he is an intelligent, happy, universally respected man.[56]

Persons are to fear God, live according to his laws, and accept life as it comes to them. Inequality of possessions or worldly goods is to be acquiesced in, for God established the social and economic order. God has made everything for the best.

Perhaps it is significant that more biblical material from Job than from any other book of the Bible is found in the Fourth Reader.[57] In these chosen passages, Job is unexcelled in faithfulness and morality—the epitome of righteousness. For that he is praised. But Job also suffers. While this appears unjust, Job insists that God is to be worshiped and adored solely because he is God. We are to be righteous simply because God wills it. We are to accept whatever happens to us in this world, for God's wisdom and kindness are beyond our comprehension. Our just reward is to know God now and to live with him forever in heaven. Happiness, especially in the next life, is a legitimate desire, but happiness in this world must never be an end in itself: "When she had learned to fear the Lord, and to honor her father and mother she was very happy." Fear God and keep your "eyes fixed on heaven" is McGuffey's advice.[58]

McGuffey's Readers may be inconsistent in their understandings of humankind, but there is no confusion as to the ultimate importance of living a moral life and the horrible price to be paid for not doing so. Every sin is an act against God, a clear demonstration that a person's heart is not right with God. Persons are eternally punished for not fearing and obeying their Creator. "Surely God has a claim to our first and principal attention." Why? Because, "If you forget God when you are young, God may forget you when you are old. It will cost something to be religious, but it will cost more not to be so."[59] The motivation for acting according to God's will and avoiding sin is also clear: a reward in eternity. Indeed, the whole purpose of life is to fear and obey God so that "we can secure his eternal friendship and be prepared for the possession of everlasting mansions in his glorious kingdom."[60]

A Christian is identified by two interrelated characteristics: a right relationship to God and right behavior. Children are admonished to "ever seek God. Pray to him when you rise, and when you lie down. Keep his day, hear his word, and do his will, and he will love you and be your God forever." Thus we are continually advised to "ask God to aid you always to do good and avoid evil"—that is, to follow a mode of piety aimed toward particular life goals and modes of conduct.[61] To those values we turn.

Value System

More than half the lessons in McGuffey's Readers have values as their dominant theme. The preferred modes of conduct are consistent with and indeed related directly to the life-goal values, and the complete value system is both a consistent and natural extension of the world view just described. Salvation and righteousness are the most frequently mentioned life goals; piety, kindness, and patriotism (in that order) the most frequently occurring preferred modes of conduct.

Life Goals

McGuffey's Readers placed salvation first among all possible terminal values, with righteousness close behind. This is not surprising. McGuffey was a Scotch-Irish

Presbyterian minister living on the midwestern frontier during the first half of the nineteenth century. It is interesting to note, however, that no previous study of the Readers mentioned their concern with salvation or righteousness. In contrast, I contend that McGuffey's Readers cannot be adequately understood without reference to the significance of these life goals.

Consider the poem "A Rest for the Weary":

> The soul, of origin divine
> God's glorious image, freed from clay,
> In heaven's eternal sphere shall shine
> A star of day!
>
> The sun is but a spark of fire,
> A transient meteor in the sky,
> The soul immortal as its sire,
> Shall never die.

At the close of this poem is a series of rhetorical questions: "Is it wise to make no preparation for death?" and "Should not our *eternal* welfare be our chief concern in this world?"[62] Of course it should. "The Bible everywhere conveys the idea that this life is not our home."[63]

Often the Readers affirm the importance of children preparing for death. "The Story of Louisa" tells of a young girl who lived a gay and merry life, indifferent to her eternal destiny. The preacher reminds her that unless she repents of her sins and asks God for forgiveness, she cannot enter heaven. Even on her death bed, while her friends read to her from the Bible and pray for her soul, she remains unmoved. The story ends sadly. Louisa dies, her body molders in the grave, and the author of the story asks, "May we not see from this story how unwise it is to put off repentance until the dying hour?"[64] All persons should realize that they were created for eternal life and that salvation should be their primary life goal.

In "The Steam Boat on Trial," Abbott tells of the construction of a new steamboat. He explains how it must be proved worthy before it is put into service. After each trial, it is improved so that at last it may fulfill its true purpose for being. Likewise, "we are on trial—on probation now. We will enter upon active service in another world."[65] To live in unity with God, to live in a right relationship to our Father in heaven, is, therefore, a life goal consistent with salvation.

"It would be a great thing to be as fine and wise and rich and glorious as King Solomon, would it not?"[66] Indeed, it would; but fine clothes and riches cannot make us happy. To be happy, we need the approval of God. To seek after his approval is to live a righteous life.

> Blessed are they which hunger and thirst after righteousness. . . . Blessed are they which are persecuted for righteousness' sake: for theirs is the kingdom of heaven. . . . For I say unto you unless your righteousness shall exceed the righteousness of the Scribes and Pharisees, ye shall in no case enter into the kingdom of heaven.[67]

A right relationship to God is understood as both religious and moral activity. To live righteously is to "love God with all your heart, mind, soul, and strength and to love your neighbor as yourself" (Mark 12:30-31). Love of God and love of neighbor go together. The lesson "Praise to God" closes with a rhetorical question: "Will God accept our praises if our conduct is not right?"[68] Of course not. Right conduct and love of God are coterminous aspects of righteousness.

Children are to live in the spirit of the psalmist:

> As the heart [*sic*] panteth after the water brooks,
> So panteth my soul after thee, O God!
> My soul thirsteth for God, for the living God.[69]

A child's motivation for righteous life is abundantly clear:

> Oh there is an hour coming, when one whisper of an approving mind, one smile of an approving God, will be accounted of more value than the wealth of a thousand worlds like this. In that hour, my young friends, nothing will sustain you, but the consciousness of having been governed in life by worthy and good principles.

Thus righteousness and salvation go together. It is better to beg for food than to "sin against God and lose your soul."[70] In this world we are to live in a conscious relationship with God, continually praising him and doing his will. In order to live such a righteous life, we must repent of our sin and accept God's grace. Then, and only then, can we act righteously and in the end be rewarded with salvation.

No other life goals are as significant as righteousness and salvation, a message consistent with the world view revealed in McGuffey's Readers and evidence of the Readers' theological presuppositions.

Modes of Conduct

Typically the values most frequently mentioned as significant in McGuffey's Readers are honesty, obedience, kindness, thrift, industry, and patriotism. Interestingly, few mention piety, the instrumental value actually found most often in the Readers. To affirm piety as a preferred mode of conduct, however, is consistent with both the world view and the life goals of salvation and righteousness that we also found in McGuffey's Readers. In one sense, all the instrumental values affirmed in the Readers are indicators of how the righteous are to live. First, and most important, is the love of God; then, love of neighbor; and last, love of country. While piety, kindness, and patriotism are central, a host of preferred modes of conduct are also found in McGuffey's Readers. Cleanliness, forgiveness, gratefulness, cooperativeness, curiosity, self-control, and meekness are all extolled. Even more important are right language, independence, courageousness, frugality, punctuality, temperance, moderation, obedience, honesty, truthfulness, love, responsibility, perseverance, learning, speaking, and humility. Those, however, that occur most frequently are charity, industriousness, patriotism, kindness, and piety.

To be charitable is to give of our abundance to aid those who cannot work, especially the sick, the elderly, and the young.

> Jane, there is a poor old man at the door.
> He asked for something to eat. We must give him some bread and cheese.
> He is cold. Will you give him some clothes too?
> I will give him a suit of old clothes which will be new to him.
> Poor man, I wish he had a warm house to live in; and kind friends to live with: then he would not have to beg from door to door.
> We should be kind to the poor. We may be poor as this old man and need as much as he.
> Shall I give him some cents to buy a pair of shoes?
> No; you may give him a pair of shoes. It is hard for the poor to have to beg from house to house.
> Poor girls and boys sometimes have to sleep out of doors all night. And when it snows they are very cold and when it rains they get wet.[71]

Another story tells of Flor Silin—a poor, hard-working Russian peasant farmer. For his industry, he is blessed with abundant crops, harvesting more than he needs. The same year the crops of the other farmers are poor. Flor Silin could be rich; instead he calls the poorest of his neighbors to his farm and addresses them: "My friends, if you want corn for your subsistence, God has blessed me with abundance—assist in thrashing out a quantity, and each of you take what he wants for his family." His poor neighbors are amazed at his generosity. Word of his benevolence travels over the land, and many famished inhabitants present themselves before him to beg for corn. He receives them all as brothers, and as long as his own abundant store remains, he shares it with those in need, saying: "It is written in the Scriptures, 'Give and it shall be given unto you.'" The following year Providence responds to the prayers and hard work of his neighbors, making their harvest abundant. Those who had been saved from starvation by Flor Silin gather around him:

"Behold," said they; "the corn you lent us. You saved our wives and children. We should have been famished but for you—may God reward you—he only can—all we have to give, is our corn and grateful thanks." "I want no corn at present, my good neighbors," said he; "my harvest has exceeded all my expectations; for the rest, thank Heaven, I have been but a humble instrument."

They urged him in vain. "No," said he, "I shall not accept your corn. If you have superfluities, share them among your poor neighbors, who, being unable to sow their fields last autumn, are still in want—let us assist them, my dear friends, the Almighty will bless us for it."[72]

Thereby, charity is extolled; we are to share our abundance with those in need. If we do not, we will be eventually punished. As "The Miser" puts it:

> Illustrious fool! Nay, most inhuman wretch!
> He sat among his bags, and, with a look
> Which hell might be ashamed of, drove the poor
> Away unalmsed, and midst abundance died,
> Sorest of evils! died of utter want.[73]

Equally as important as charity is industriousness. "John Jones" tells of a good boy who could not read or write because his mother was too poor to send him to school. Instead, John worked hard, breaking stones by the side of the road. Of course, he did not earn much at this labor, but it was morally good for him to work. It is good for all of us to be industrious; it is wrong for us to be idle. "John was a good boy and he did not love to play so much that he could not work. No! He knew it to be right to work and when his work was done, he could play."[74]

"The Little Idle Boy" and "The Idle Boy Reformed" communicate a similar message. Of the little idle boy, we are told that one day he sees a bee flying from one flower to another. He asks the pretty bee to come play with him, but the bee responds, "No, I must not be idle, I must go and gather honey." He meets a dog. He wants the dog to play with him, but the dog says that he must not be idle; he must catch a hare for his master's dinner. The little boy finds a bird and asks the bird to play. Again, the bird says, "No: I must not be idle; I must build a nest." Last, the boy sees a horse, and he asks the horse to play with him. But the horse says, "No, I must not be idle; I must plow the field." Then the little boy thinks to himself, "Is nobody idle? Then little boys must not be idle." [75]

"The Truant" is about a boy who sleeps late and, when he wakes, goes back to sleep again. He is idle and worthless. Because of this idleness he is ignorant, falls into crime, and has no friends. The lesson concludes: "Wretched are the parents of such a son, grief and shame are theirs, his name shall be stamped with the mark of infamy when their poor broken hearts shall moulder in the grave." [76]

"The Good Boy Whose Parents Are Poor" tells of a poor boy who rises early each morning to help his father and mother. He walks quickly to school so that he doesn't waste any time. In school he is very good and studies hard. As a result he learns how to read the Bible and other good books. When he finishes his lessons, he doesn't stop to play. Rather, he runs home to help his parents. When he is home he is very industrious. He takes care of his brothers and his sisters, weeds the garden, and sometimes works with his father. Because of his industry, he is very happy and indeed glad that he can work, because he hopes that some day he will be able to earn the money to buy his own clothes and food. Often he sees little boys and girls in fine clothes riding on pretty horses or walking with ladies and gentlemen, but he never envies them. Instead he philosophizes:

> I have often been told and I have read, that it is God who makes some poor, and others rich;—that the rich have many troubles which we know nothing of; and that the poor if they are but good, may be very happy: indeed, I think that when I am good, nobody can be happier than I am. [77]

"The Advantage of Industry" points out that many young people seem to think that it is of little consequence if they use their time well. Some realize that it is disgraceful for men and women to be idle, but they believe there is no harm

in the young spending their time in any manner they please.
The lesson challenges this contention by stating clearly that
unless people work hard when they are young, they will
never achieve. Why? Because the habits we learn when
young go with us. Unless we are industrious as children, we
will never be industrious when we grow up. The lesson then
closes by telling of George Jones and the price he paid for
being idle:

> A few months ago, I met him a poor wanderer, without
> money and without friends. Such are the wages of idleness. I
> hope every reader will from this history take warning. . . .
> The story of George Jones, which is a true one, shows how
> sinful and ruinous it is to be idle. Every child who would be a
> Christian, and have a home in heaven, must guard against this
> sin.[78]

McGuffey's Readers make especially clear that charity
and industriousness are God's will, but the three most
significant modes of conduct in the eyes of God are
patriotism, kindness, and piety; we are instructed to love
God, neighbor, and country.

Love of country is understood as a religious act. America
is a gift from God. We are God's holy nation, his blessed
people. "Happy Consequences of American Independence"
confesses that no nation under heaven enjoys so much
happiness as America. Therefore,

> let us consider God as the author of all our blessings,
> acknowledging him as our beneficent parent, protector, and
> friend. While we celebrate the anniversary of our indepen-
> dence let us remember that: A voice from the altar cries,
> "these are they who loved their country, these are they who
> died for liberty." We now reap the fruit of their agony and
> toil. Let their memories be eternally embalmed in our
> bosoms.[79]

In a two-part lesson on the necessity of education,
Beecher comments upon how God brought our fathers to
this land to lay the foundations of religious liberty and how
God preserved us by raising up patriots to continue his

work. To this day, therefore, "true lovers of the virtue of patriotism contemplate its purest models."[80] And among the purest, George Washington stands out above all the rest. The Readers call upon all citizens to emulate his patriotic spirit. As Webster put it, "Let us trust in that gracious Being who has held our country in the hollow of his hand." Love of God and love of country belong together. Patriotism acknowledges God's provident action in creating our country. We are God's chosen people.

Perhaps, most significant is the juxtaposition of the two lessons at the end of the Fourth Reader. First, we find a passage from the Book of Revelation, "The Celestial City," which tells of God's action to establish a new heaven and a new earth; immediately following is Mason's "America—National Hymn." America witnesses to God's new creation.

Love of neighbor, or kindness, is also extolled. Kindness in McGuffey's Readers is directed toward all God's creatures. In the First Reader, "The School Girl" praises Jane Rice who, going to school, finds a poor bee in the water and saves its life, and "The Kind Boy" praises James Bland who, finding a poor young bird unable to care for itself, cares for it and, when the bird is well, sets it free.

But kindness is also a loving concern for people. "The Way To Be Happy" explains:

> Do all in your power to make others happy. Be willing to make sacrifices of your own convenience that you may promote the happiness of others. . . .
> When you are playing with your brothers and sisters at home, be always ready to give them more than their store of privileges. Manifest an obliging disposition, and they cannot but regard you with affection. In all your intercourse with others, at home and abroad, let these feelings influence you, and you will receive a rich reward.[81]

"Christ and the Blind Man" gives scriptural support for love of neighbor, but it should be noted that kindness is never concerned with justice. In every case, kindness is individualistic, personalistic, and patronizing. To be kind is to be friendly. To love one's neighbor is to give of one's abundance to those in need. For example, in the First Reader we have the story of "The Lame Man" in which a child is told it is good to give a bit of his cake and milk to the sick, old, poor man. In "Little Henry," which follows, the child is again encouraged to give a share of his cake to the old man who could not see to work.

A story in the Second Reader entitled "The Kind Little Girl" is about a five-year-old child who was good and kind to all. Because of that everyone was fond of her. Even the beasts and the birds around the house would come when they heard her voice. One day she sat down by a fence. A poor thin dog came to her. She saw the dog's need and gave him a small bit of her cake. Then an old man came out of his hut to call the dog. She saw that he was old, thin, pale, and sick, and she gave him a large piece of her cake. Then the lesson makes an interesting comment: if the man or the dog had been young, fat, healthy, and strong, she would not have thought of sharing her cake or giving them a bite to eat. It was only because they were in special need that she knew that it was her duty to give them a small part of what she had.

In the Second Reader there is another interesting lesson on kindness that tells of two boys who were always competing to see who should be the very best in their class. One was wealthy, the other poor. The academic race was nip and tuck. Then one day the poor boy did not come to school, because his widowed mother no longer could afford to send him. The other boy, a rich farmer's son, aware of his rival's need, took some of his allowance and paid the tuition. In the story, the poor boy returns to school and ends up at the head of the class. But it is the boy who was kind that is praised.

Love country, love neighbor; both are important, but the most frequently mentioned instrumental value in the McGuffey Readers is piety. "Evening Prayer" commends:

At the close of day before you go to sleep, you should not fail to pray to God to keep you from sin and from harm.
You ask your friends for food, and drink, and books, and

clothes; and when they give you these things you thank them, and love them for the good they do you.

So should you ask your God for those things which he can give you, which no one else can give you.

You should ask him for life and strength and health; and you should pray to him to keep your feet from the ways of sin and shame.

You should thank him for all his good gifts; and learn, while young, to put your trust in him; and the kind care of God will be with you, both in youth and in your old age.[82]

Lessons on piety—fear, love, and gratitude to God—are found throughout the Readers. For example:

I hope you have said your prayers and thanked your Father in heaven for all his goodness. I hope you have thanked him for your good health, and the blessings of a home, for your kind parents, for tender friends, for pleasant books, and for all other enjoyments.

Never forget, before you leave your room to thank God for his kindness. He is indeed kinder to us than an earthly parent.

Let us now go out of doors. How beautiful the sun rises upon the hills! How glorious a thing is the sun, and how much like that Being who dwells in the Heavens, sending down his mercies upon mankind, as the sun sheds its light and its warmth upon the world![83]

If pious behavior is a proper way to begin the day, the same is appropriate at its close:

Before we close our eyes, let us lift up our hearts in gratitude to that Great Being who never sleeps, but watches over us as a shepherd watching over his flock. . . .

Above all let us ask God to fill our hearts with love for him; to inspire us with love of everything that is good, and to refrain from everything that is evil. Let us ask him to let us love to tell the truth, and be ashamed to tell a lie.

Let us ask him to watch over us in our sleep when darkness is around us and none but he is awake to keep us from evil.[84]

A nature story entitled "About the Stars" exclaims:

We must often think of the Lord who is so great and good. We must love him with all our hearts, and try to do his will.

Let us look up to him with love and praise, and indulge in
the hope, that when we leave this earth, he will take us to
heaven, where we may study the stars, and learn all the
glorious things that he has done.[85]

Sprague's poem "The Winged Worshipers" is addressed
to two swallows that flew into church one Sunday during
worship. The author laments—

> Ye never knew
> The crimes for which we come to weep:
> Penance is not for you,
> Bless'd wand'rers of the upper deep.

and then envies—

> To you 'tis given
> To wake sweet nature's untaught lays;
> Beneath the arch of heaven
> To chirp away a life of praise.[86]

"True Wisdom," an excerpt from the Bible, closes—
"Behold! the fear of the Lord, that is wisdom," and a poem
by Hannah More exclaims:

> Minds drawn thitherward and closely linked
> In the celestial union; 'tis in this
> Sweet element alone, that we can live
> To any purpose.

In the same spirit we find in Psalm 148, "Joyous Devotion,"
a hymn of praise to God, praise that ought to be on the lips
of all his people.[87]

In the final lines of an essay on human life, Samuel
Johnson writes, "Go now, my son, to thy repose; commit
thyself to the care of Omnipotence; and, when the morning
calls again to toil, begin thy journey and thy life."
Correspondingly, Erskine closes "Paine's Age of Reason"
with these words:

> Thus, gentlemen, you find all that is great or wise, or
> splendid, or illustrious, among created beings, all the minds
> gifted beyond ordinary nature, if not inspired by their

Universal Author for the advancement and dignity of the world, though divided by distant ages, and by the clashing opinions which distinguish them from one another, yet joining, as it were in one sublime chorus to celebrate the truths of Christianity, and laying upon its holy altars the never-fading offering of their immortal wisdom.[88]

A story about the Icelanders states that the most important characteristic and trait of these people is their piety. The lesson explains that when the Icelanders awaken, they do not salute any person but hasten to the door and, lifting up their eyes toward heaven, adore him who made the heavens and the earth, the author and preserver of their being and the source of every blessing. Only then do they return into the house to greet those they meet with "God grant you a good day."[89]

Basically, the McGuffey Readers directed persons to live for salvation—for eternal life with God in another world—a life goal closely connected to righteousness. The modes of conduct most expressive of righteousness are love of country, love of neighbor, and love of God. It is the last value—piety—that is most important, for indeed all the others depend upon it.

The Northwest Ordinance of 1787 stated that "religion, morality and knowledge are necessary to good government and the happiness of mankind." McGuffey's Readers supported that contention and provided a resource for the education of Christians. First religion, then morality, and last knowledge—that was the focus of their content.

We should not be surprised, therefore, to learn that McGuffey's Readers read more like a theology textbook than a children's elementary schoolbook. Life is God-conscious and God-centered in McGuffey's Readers. The Bible is crucial for understanding God as creator, preserver, and governor, and for understanding his will. The natural world, which can be understood properly only in relation to God, is orderly, beautiful, and good. We, who also can be understood properly only in relation to God, are to live in harmony with nature and act as stewards of God's creation. Nevertheless, this world is not ultimate, for we are children of eternity. While we are born in sin and destined to damnation, God, in Christ, reconciles those who repent to himself and rewards them with eternal life. Salvation and righteousness are therefore life goals of the faithful.

That, simply, is the theistic world view and value system of McGuffey's Readers. It is a view and system of values not always emphasized by commentators of McGuffey's Readers, but it is worthy of the Scotch-Irish Presbyterian minister who compiled them and the children of the Middle Border who attended our early nineteenth-century common schools.

Later Editions

While the purpose of this book is not to present a detailed content analysis of the 1879 edition or a full comparison with the 1836–37 editions, a few summary findings need to be shared. Few lessons from the 1836–37 editions are to be found in the 1879 edition. There are none in the First Reader. Only "The Greedy Girl" (from the First Reader of 1836) remains in the Second Reader. "True Courage," "The Truant," "Things to Remember," "The Lord's Prayer," "Young Soldier" (all from the Second Reader), and "Evening Prayer" (from the First) are found in the Third Reader. "The Consequences of Idleness," "The Advantages of Industry," and "The Lost Child" by Abbott; "The Old Oaken Bucket" by Woodworth; and "The Sermon on the Mount" are found in the Fourth Reader. The theistic world view, so dominant in the 1836–37 edition, slowly disappears. God is mentioned more rarely: in one lesson in the 1879 edition of the First Reader, in two lessons of the Second Reader, in four lessons of the Third Reader, and in just ten lessons of the Fourth Reader. While each of the 1836–37 editions contains numerous stories from the Bible, the Sermon on the Mount and the Protestant version of the

Lord's Prayer are the only pieces of scripture to remain in the 1879 edition.

None of the first edition emphasis on salvation and piety remains. In their place is a morality of industry, self-denial, sobriety, thrift, propriety, persistence, modesty, punctuality, conformity, and submission to authority. The spirit of self-reliance, individualism, and competition fill the 1879 edition. Virtue is rarely its own reward, but material and physical rewards can be expected for good acts. Likewise wickedness will be punished. It is hard work and frugality that bring prosperity. Responsibility for success or failure lies with the individual. No matter how bad life may appear, however, persons should be satisfied with their lot and not be distressed over any present social, political, or economic arrangements. Still, the affluent should use their wealth in socially responsible ways.

The 1879 edition of the First Reader has few characteristics of the 1836 edition; closest is the following lesson:

> See my dear, old grandma is in her easy chair! How gray her hair is! She wears glasses when she reads.
>
> She is always kind, and takes such good care of me that I like to do what she tells me.
>
> When she says, "Robert, will you get me a drink?" I run as fast as I can to get it for her. Then she says, "Thank you, my boy."
>
> Would you not love a dear, good grandma, who is so kind? And would you not do all you could to please her?[90]

The Second Reader primarily affirms the values of kindness, honesty, obedience to elders, and hard work. Those who live by such values will be rewarded, those who do not will be punished. Pleasure is depreciated: "I am glad you have learned that there may be something more pleasant than play, and, at the same time more instructive."[91] The only lesson that comes close to the character of those in the 1836 edition reads:

> I know God made the Sun
> To fill the day with light.

He made the twinkling stars
   To shine all through the night.

He made the hills that rise
   So very high and steep.
He made the lakes and seas
   That are so broad and deep.

He made each bird that sings
   So sweetly all the day.
He made each flower that springs
   So bright, so fresh, so gay.

And He who made all these
   He made both you and me.
Oh, let us thank Him, then
   For great and good is He.[92]

Like the Second Reader, the Third (1879) affirms rural small-town life. It especially lauds hard work, self-help, and perseverance: "If your castles get knocked down, build them up again."[93] Obedience to one's elders is rewarded, so are honesty, kindness, and especially labor.

God is mentioned more frequently in the Third Reader, but typically in this way:

At night, before you go to sleep, think whether you have done anything that was wrong during the day, and pray to God to forgive you. If any one has done you wrong, forgive him in your heart.

If you have not learned something useful, or been in some way useful, during the past day, think that it is a day lost, and be very sorry for it.

Trust in the Lord, and He will guide you in the way of good men. The path of the just is as the shining light that shineth more and more unto the perfect day.

We must do all the good we can to all men, for this is well pleasing in the sight of God. He delights to see his children walk in love and do good one to another.[94]

One lesson on the evils of alcohol can be found, but more typical is a lesson on charity that ends: "Now, I thought to myself, 'Mary Williams, you have had a good breakfast and a good dinner this day, and this poor girl has not had a mouthful. You can give her your dinner; she needs it a great deal more than you do.'"[95]

The Fourth Reader (1879) refers to God much more frequently than the other three, but like them it speaks of God as creator and judge, rewarder and punisher. The lessons, however, in general present a gospel of success—all have the opportunity for riches and happiness if they strive and persevere; if they are industrious, loyal to their employers, frugal, and reliable; and if they live virtuous lives. At the same time no one is to covet another's riches, for "God makes everybody rich."[96] There are no stories of rebels, reformers, dissenters, pilgrims, or seekers.

Typical of the stories in the Fourth Reader is "Dare to Do Right," which was adopted from Thomas Hughes' *School Days at Rugby*. It is a story about a young man who dared to pray before going to bed in spite of the negative reactions from his classmates. It is also a story of how his steadfastness led others to act as they knew was right.

Most usual, however, is a lesson entitled "The Golden Rule." Beginning with the dictum "whatsoever you would that men should do to you, do you even so with them," it explains this command in terms of the parable of the Good Samaritan. The story focuses on temptation and the personal satisfaction and reward for living according to the Golden Rule.

A detailed content analysis of the 1850 and 1879 editions of McGuffey's Readers is needed if we are to understand the history of these important textbooks. What is most important for our purposes, however, is an awareness of the uniqueness of the 1836–37 editions of the Readers and of William H. McGuffey's mind and spirit. McGuffey made an important contribution to American history and education. His true significance needs to be understood and acknowledged. As a representative of Protestants living on the Middle Border in the early nineteenth century, McGuffey helps us to comprehend the changing history of our nation and to better understand our forebears' concern for piety, morality, and education.

Notes

1. Frederick Streng, *Understanding Religious Man* (Belmont, Cal.: Dickenson Publishing Co., 1969), p. 25.
2. W. H. McGuffey, *Eclectic First Reader* and *Eclectic Second Reader* (Cincinnati: Truman & Smith, 1836); *Eclectic Third Reader* and *Eclectic Fourth Reader* (Cincinnati: Truman & Smith, 1837). Notes will cite chapter title, the Reader, and page number.
3. "More about the Little Chimney Sweep," *First*, p. 66.
4. "The Poor Old Man," p. 13; "The Sun Is Up," p. 25; "The Thick Shade," 29; "More about the Little Boy Who Told a Lie," p. 63; "John Jones," p. 33, all in *First*.
5. See "The Bible.—Grimke," *Fourth*, p. 159; "John Jones," *First*, p. 33; "The Bible.—Tyng," *Third*, p. 56; "Gospel Invitation.—Isaiah LV," *Third*, p. 162.
6. "Ode from the 19th Psalm.—Addison," *Third*, p. 115.
7. See "How the World Was Made," *Second*, p. 81.
8. "Story of George Washington," *Second*, p. 130.
9. See "Clothing of Animals and Vegetables.—Flint," p. 68; "The Rainbow," p. 73; both in *Third*.
10. "The Poor Old Man," *First*, p. 13.
11. "Time to Get Up," *Second*, p. 10.
12. "About the Globe," *Second*, p. 112.
13. "John Jones," p. 32; "The Poor Old Man," p. 13, both in *First*.
14. "Character of Martin Luther.—Robertson," *Third*, p. 125.
15. "Remarkable Preservation.—Prof. Wilson," *Fourth*, pp. 14, 17.
16. "The Deluge.—Bible," pp. 114-15; "Death of Absalom.—Bible," p. 43, both in *Fourth*.
17. "Settlement of America," *Second*, p. 152.
18. "Happy Consequences of American Independence.—Maxey," *Fourth*, p. 185.
19. "On the Being of God.—Young," *Fourth*, p. 133.
20. "The Thick Shade," *First*, p. 29.
21. "Benevolence of the Supreme Being.—Chalmers," *Fourth*, p. 184.
22. "The Sun Is Up," *First*, p. 15.
23. "Omnipresence of God.—Bible," *Fourth*, p. 199.
24. "Happy Consequences of American Independence.—Maxey," *Fourth*, p. 184.
25. "About the Moon," p. 35; "The Thick Shade," p. 29, both in *First*. See also "The Sun Is Up," *First*, p. 15.
26. "Evening Prayer," *First*, p. 59.
27. "An End of All Perfection.—Signourney," *Fourth*, p. 88.
28. See "The Cat and the Dog," *First*, p. 9.
29. "The Way to Be Happy," *Third*, pp. 24, 25.
30. "Don't Take Strong Drink," *First*, p. 67.

31. "The Alps.—W. Gaylord Clark," p. 180; "God's First Temples.—Bryant," pp. 52, 53, both in *Fourth*.
32. "God's First Temples," *Fourth*, p. 55.
33. "Works of the Coral Insect.—Univ. Review," *Third*, pp. 116, 117.
34. "The Thunder Storm.—Scrap Book," *Third*, p. 43.
35. "Reverie," *Western Monthly Magazine*, May, 1838, pp. 22, 23.
36. "The Steam Boat on Trial.—Abbott," *Fourth*, pp. 134, 137.
37. "Thought in a Place of Public Worship.—Hannah Moore," *Fourth*, p. 192.
38. "More about Joseph," *Second*, p. 143.
39. "On Speaking the Truth.—Abbott," *Third*, pp. 89, 90.
40. *Ibid.*, p. 91.
41. "Necessity of Education.—Beecher," *Fourth*, p. 60.
42. "The Bible.—Tyng," *Third*, p. 56.
43. "Midnight Musings.—Young," *Fourth*, p. 198.
44. "The Little Readers," *Second*, p. 10.
45. "Differences Between Man and the Inferior Animals.—Jane Taylor," *Third*, p. 141.
46. "Value of Time and Knowledge.—Hawes," *Third*, p. 121.
47. "The Advantages of Reading.—Hawes," *Third*, p. 92.
48. "Contrasted Soliloquies.—Taylor," *Fourth*, p. 22.
49. "The Lost Child.—Abbott," *Third*, p. 71.
50. "The Ten Commandments," *Second*, p. 169; "Gospel Invitation.—Bible," *Third*, p. 69.
51. "Character of the Puritan Fathers of New England.—Greenwood," *Fourth*, p. 125.
52. "Things to Remember," *Second*, p. 156.
53. "The Consequences of Idleness.—Abbott," p. 18; "The Advantages of Industry.—Abbott," p. 20, both in *Third*.
54. "The Miser.—Pollok," *Fourth*, p. 220.
55. "Love of Applause.—Hawes," *Fourth*, pp. 148, 149.
56. See "The Consequences of Idleness" and "The Advantages of Industry."
57. "Vision of a Spirit," p. 122; "Divine Providence," p. 140; "Scripture Lesson," p. 150; "True Wisdom," p. 221; "Portrait of a Patriarch.—Addison," p. 85, all in *Fourth*.
58. "More about the Disobedient Girl," *Second*, p. 122; "Decisive Integrity.—Wirt," *Fourth*, p. 130.
59. "The Importance of a Well Spent Youth," p. 155; "Short Sentences.—Mason," p. 54, both in *Third*.
60. "More about the Bible," *Third*, p. 60.
61. "John Jones," p. 33; "Good Advice," p. 50, both in *First*.
62. "A Rest for the Weary.—Montgomery," *Fourth*, p. 91.
63. "The Steam Boat on Trial.—Abbott," *Fourth*, p. 134. See also "More about Joseph," *Second*, 143.
64. "The Story of Louisa.—Abbott," *Third*, p. 133.
65. "The Steam Boat on Trial.—Abbott," *Third*, p. 137.
66. "More about King Solomon," *Second*, p. 54.
67. "Sermon on the Mount.—Bible," *Third*, pp. 80-81.
68. "Praise to God," *Second*, p. 61.

69. "Thirsting after Righteousness.—Bible," *Fourth*, p. 174.
70. "Love of Applause.—Hawes," *Fourth*, p. 149.
71. "The Poor Old Man," *First*, p. 12.
72. "The Generous Russian Peasant.—Karamsin," *Third*, pp. 139, 140.
73. "The Miser.—Pollok," *Fourth*, p. 220.
74. "John Jones," *First*, p. 32.
75. "The Idle Boy Reformed," *Second*, pp. 12-13.
76. "The Truant," *Second*, p. 43.
77. "The Good Boy Whose Parents Are Poor," *Second*, p. 45.
78. "The Consequences of Idleness.—Abbott," *Third*, p. 18.
79. "Happy Consequences of American Independence.—Maxey," *Fourth*, p. 184.
80. "Washington's Birth Day.—Webster," *Fourth*, p. 66.
81. "The Way To Be Happy.—Child at Home," *Third*, p. 26.
82. "Evening Prayer," *First*, pp. 59-60.
83. "Time To Get Up," *Second*, pp. 10-11.
84. "Time To Go To Bed," *Second*, p. 25.
85. "About the Stars," *Second*, p. 27.
86. "The Winged Worshipers.—Sprague," *Fourth*, p. 37.
87. "True Wisdom.—Bible," *Fourth*, p. 221; "Thoughts in a Place of Worship.—More," *Fourth*, p. 192; "Joyous Devotion.—Bible," *Fourth*, p. 101.
88. "The Journey of a Day.—Dr. Johnson," *Fourth*, p. 313; "Paine's Age of Reason.—Erskine," *Fourth*, p. 139.
89. "The Character of Icelanders.—Henderson," *Fourth*, p. 99.
90. *First* (1879), pp. 51-52.
91. "The Fire Side," *Second*, p. 72.
92. "God is Great and Good," *Second*, (1879), pp. 119-20.
93. "Castle Building," *Third*, (1879), p. 25.
94. "Things To Remember," *Third*, (1879), pp. 66-67.
95. "Mary's Dime," *Third*, (1879), p. 169.
96. "Harry's Riches," *Fourth*, (1879), p. 77.

CHAPTER IV

Exemplary Lessons from McGuffey's Readers

On the following pages are representative lessons from the first editions of the Readers. The title page and complete table of contents from each of the four Readers is also included. While each of these lessons is typical of the first editions of the Readers, none are found in the most popular and still available 1879 edition.

The following exemplary lessons represent material from the only edition personally compiled by William Holmes McGuffey and therefore include material from:

McGuffey, W. H. *Eclectic First Reader*. Cincinnati: Truman & Smith, 1836.

McGuffey, W. H. *Eclectic Second Reader*. Cincinnati: Truman & Smith, 1836.

McGuffey, W. H. *Eclectic Third Reader*. Cincinnati: Truman & Smith, 1837.

McGuffey, W. H. *Eclectic Fourth Reader*. Cincinnati: Truman & Smith, 1837.

McGUFFEY'S ECLECTIC FIRST READER

CONTENTS*

CONTENTS

---

*The first edition of the First Reader did not have a table of contents. The contents of the Reader are listed here for reference.

THE

ECLECTIC FIRST READER,

FOR

YOUNG CHILDREN.

CONSISTING OF

PROGRESSIVE LESSONS

IN

READING AND SPELLING

MOSTLY IN

EASY WORDS OF ONE AND TWO SYLLABLES.

BY W. H. M'GUFFEY,

Professor in the Miami University, Oxford, Ohio.

CINCINNATI:
PUBLISHED BY TRUMAN AND SMITH,
150, MAIN STREET.
1837.

LESSON X.

The Sun is Up.

See, the sun is up. The sun gives us light. It makes the trees and the grass grow.

The sun rises in the east and sets in the west. When the sun rises, it is day.

When the sun sets it is night.

This little boy was up at five. He saw the sun rise, and heard the sweet songs of birds on every bush.

Do you know who made the sun ?

God made it.

God made the moon and all the stars. How good God is to us ; he gives us all we have, and keeps us alive.

We should love God.

God sees and knows all things, for God is every where. He sees me when I rise from my bed, when I go out to walk and play. And when I lie down to sleep at night, he keeps me from harm.

Though I do not see the wind, yet it blows round me on all sides : so God is with me at all times, and yet I see him not.

If God is with me, and knows all that I do, he must hear what I say. O, let me not, then, speak bad words ; for if I do, God will not love me.

sun	grass	should	must
light	then	makes	hear
birds	things	knows	east
lit-tle	boy	all	five
sweet	birds	ev-e-ry	bush
God	sees	when	rise
how	play	sides	sleep
hear	though	times	say
keeps	harm	speak	words

LESSON XVIII.

The Thick Shade.

Come, let us go into the thick shade, for it is noon-day, and the summer sun beats hot upon our heads.

The shade is pleasant and cool ; the branches meet above our heads and shut out the sun as with a green curtain.

The grass is soft to our feet, and the clear brook washes the roots of the trees.

The cattle can lie down to sleep in the cool shade, but we can do better ; we can

raise our voices to heaven; we can prai
the great God who made us.

He made the warm sun and th co
shade; the trees that grow upwards, ar
the brooks that run along.

The plants and trees are made to gi
fruit to man.

All that live get life from God. H
made the poor man, as well as the ric
man.

He made the dark man, as well as tl
fair man. He made the fool, as well a
the wise man. All that move on the lar
are his; and so all that fly in the air, ar
all that swim in the sea.

The ox and the worm are both the wor
of his hand. In him they live and mov
He it is that doth give food to them all, an
when he says the word, they all must di

come	noon	in-to	thick
shade	trees	day	heat
heads	clear	cool	branch-e
soft	down	brook	up ward
cat-tle	voi-ces	sleep	bet-ter
raise	pleas-ant	heav-en	sum-me

LESSON XX.

John Jones.

John Jones was a good boy, but he could not read nor write. His mother was poor and could not pay for him to go to school: so she sent him out to help a man at the side of the road to break stones. John could not earn much, it is true, yet it was good for him to be at work.

It is well for us all to have work to do. It is bad for us not to work. John was a good boy, and he did not love to play so much that he could not work. No—he knew it to be right to work, and when his work was done he would play.

The man for whom John worked was very kind to John, and gave him a great deal of good advice.

One day he said to him, "John, you must always bear in mind, that it was God who made you, and who gave you all that you have, and all that you hope for. He gave you life, and food, and a home to live in.

All who take care of you and help you,

were sent you by God. He sent his Son, to show you his will, and to die for your sake.

He gave you his word, to let you know what he hath done for you, and what he bids you do.

Be sure that he sees you, in the dark, as well as in the day light. He can tell all that you do, and all that you say, and all that is in your mind.

Oh ! ever seek this God. Pray to him when you rise, and when you lie down. Keep his day, hear his word, and do his will, and he will love you, and will be your God for ever."

~~~~~~~~

have	you	hope	hath
pray	die	word	help
done	life	sent	read
food	bear	that	mind
your	live	whom	ev-er
work-ed	good	show	dark
very	ad-vice	day	light
kind	al-ways	know	seek
great	some	him	deal
gave	sees	down	hope

LESSON XXXVII.

Evening Prayer.

At the close of the day, before you go to sleep, you should not fail to pray to God to keep you from sin and from harm.

You ask your friends for food, and drink, and books, and clothes; and when they give you these things, you thank them, and love them for the good they do you.

So you should ask your God for those things which he can give you, and which no one else can give you.

You should ask him for life, and health,

and strength ; and you should pray to him
to keep your feet from the ways of sin and
shame.

You should thank him for all his good
gifts ; and learn, while young, to put your
trust in him ; and the kind care of God
will be with you, both in your youth and in
your old age.

~~~~~~~~

close	before	sleep	would
fail	pray	from	harm
friends	food	drink	books
clothes	these	things	them
good	should	those	which
strength	learn	young	youth

LESSON XLII.

Don't Take Strong Drink.

No little boy or girl should ever drink rum or whisky, unless they want to become drunkards.

Men who drink strong drink are glad to have any excuse for doing it. So, one will drink it because he is so hot. Another will drink it because he is cold.

One will drink it when he is wet, and another because he is dry—one will drink it because he is in company, and another, because he is alone, and another will put it into his glass of water to kill the insects!

Thus the pure water from the brook is poisoned with the "drunkard's drink," and the man who uses it, becomes a sot. Then he is seen tottering through the streets, a shame to himself and to all his family.

And oh, how dreadful to die a drunkard. The Bible says that no drunkard shall inherit the kingdom of heaven.

Whiskey makes the happy miserable, and it causes the rich to become poor.

THE

ECLECTIC SECOND READER;

CONSISTING OF

PROGRESSIVE LESSONS

IN

READING AND SPELLING.

FOR THE

YOUNGER CLASSES IN SCHOOLS.

WITH ENGRAVINGS.

BY W. H. M'GUFFEY,

PROFESSOR IN MIAMI UNIVERSITY, OXFORD.

STEREOTYPE EDITION.

CINCINNATI:
PUBLISHED BY TRUMAN AND SMITH,
150 MAIN STREET.

CONTENTS.

CONTENTS.

LESSON XIII.

Time to go to Bed.

1. It is evening. The sun is setting behind the mountains, and the shadows begin to darken the forests.

2. The birds have ceased to sing, except a lonely robin or a thrush, that sits upon the top of a tree, and sings a plaintive hymn.

3. The farmer has left the field and is going to his happy home ; the bee is silent in the hive. The buzzing insects are still, and the fowls, who, a little while since, were filling the air with their notes, are heard no more.

4. All around us seem to seek repose, and the very hills and valleys appear to be sinking into gentle sleep. We too must now retire to our pillows.

5. Before we close our eyes, let us lift up our hearts in gratitude to that Great Being who never sleeps, but watches over us, as the shepherd watches over his flock.

6. Let us ask his forgiveness for our faults and his aid to avoid every sin. Let us seek his friendship, and ask him to assist us to be kind and amiable to our brothers and sisters, and companions ;——to be gentle to every living thing ; to obey and love our parents ; to respect the aged ; and to be kind to the sick and to the poor.

7. Above all, let us ask God to fill our hearts with love for him; to inspire us with a love of every thing that is good, and to refrain from every thing that is evil. Let us ask him to

make us love to tell the truth, and to be ashamed to tell a lie.

8. Let us ask him to watch over us in our sleep when darkness is around us, and none but he is awake to keep us from evil.

Questions.—1. What part of the day is it when the birds cease to sing? 2. Who is it that keeps the Birds and the Bees alive when they are asleep? 3. Who takes care of you when you are asleep? 4. Ought you to love him, and serve him while you are awake?

watch	e-ven-ing	set-ting	re-frain
friend	shad-ows	dark-en	for-est
done	ceas-ed	ex-cept	lone-ly
keep	rob-in	fill-ing	re-pose
safe-ly	ap-pear	a-sham-ed	sink-ing
re-sign	in-spire	mount-ains	dark-ness
val-leys	con-fi-dence	what-ev-er	pro-tec-tor
be-fore	grat-i-tude	our-selves	daugh-ters

LESSON XXXIII.

Praise to God.

1. Come, let us praise God, for he is exceedingly great; let us bless God, for he is very good.

2. He made all things; the sun to rule the day; the moon to shine by night.

3. He made the great whale, and the elephant; and the little worm that crawleth upon the ground.

4. The little birds sing praises to God, when they warble sweetly in the green shade.

5. The brooks and rivers praise God, when they murmur melodiously amongst the smooth pebbles.

6. I will praise God with my voice ; for I may praise him, though I am but a little child.

7. A few years ago, and I was but a little infant, and my tongue was dumb within my mouth.

8. And I did not know the great name of God, for my reason was not come unto me.

9. But I can now speak, and my tongue shall praise him : I can think of all his kindness, and my heart shall love him.

10. Let him call me, and I will come unto him; let him command, and I will obey him.

11. When I am older, I will praise him better; and I will never forget God, so long as my life remaineth in me.

Questions.—1. What is the subject of this lesson ? 2. Who made the sun, and moon, and all things that live upon the earth ? 3. Who is it that has protected you from harm, and now keeps you alive ? 4. Will God listen to the praises of little children ? 5. Should you not, then, praise God for his

goodness to you ? 6. Will God accept our praises if our c⸸
duct is not right ?

great	think	for-get	mur-mu⸸
praise	great	bet-ter	peb-ble⸸
heart	whale	nev-er	in-fant
dumb	smooth	ver-y	a-mong
mouth	tongue	old-er	war-ble⸸

re-main-eth	el-e-phant	crawl-e⸸
kind-ness	me-lo-di-ous-ly	for-get
com-mand	ex-ceed-ing-ly	rea-so⸸
mur-mur	re-main-eth	glo-ry

LESSON LXXXI.

Things to Remember.

1. Remember, child, remember,
That God is in the sky,
That he looks on all we do
With an ever wakeful eye.

2. Remember, oh! remember,
That all the day and night,
He sees our thoughts and actions,
With an ever watchful sight.

3. Remember, child, remember,
That God is good and true ;
That he wishes us to be
Like him in all we do.

4. Remember that he hates
A falsehood or a lie—
Remember, he will punish
The wicked by-and-bye.

5. Remember, oh! remember,
That he is like a friend,
And he wishes us to be
Good, and happy in the end.

6. Remember, child, remember
To pray to him in heaven ;
And if you have done wrong,
Oh! ask to be forgiven.

7. Be sorry, in your little prayer,
And whisper in his ear ;
Ask his forgiveness and his love,
And he will surely hear :

8. Yes, he will hear thee, and forgive
Like a father, good and kind ;
So remember, child, remember,
That you love with all your mind—

9. The God, who lives in heaven,
And gives us each delight,
Who guards us all the day,
And saves us in the night.

Questions.—1. Who is it that looks on all we do? 2. Ca
God see us in the dark? 3. What does God hate? 4. Wh
must we remember to do, if we have done wrong? 6. Wh
will forgive us? 6. Whom must we love with all our hearts

for-give	fa-ther	ac-tions
wish-es	sure-ly	watch-ful
heav-en	de-light	re-mem-ber

LESSON LXXXIV.
About Using Profane Language.

1. All children know what is meant by profane swearing ; yet, but few understand the nature and extent of the guilt incurred by it.

2. If any of you had a very dear friend, who had bestowed many valuable gifts upon you, and to whom you felt the warmest gratitude, and who was entitled to your most profound respect on account of his moral excellencies of character ; you would not use the name of that friend in a disrespectful manner, nor could you hear it so by another, without the greatest pain.

3. It would be base ingratitude in *you*, to use it lightly ; and he would have but little regard. for your feelings, who would thus use it in your presence.

4. But God has been kinder to us than *all* our earthly friends. He has bestowed upon us such favors as we can never hope to return, or confer upon any others ; gratitude is the only return we can make.

5. He is the very *fountain* of all moral excellence, and therefore can never be sufficiently venerated. Will you then, my young reader treat God as you would not treat a friend ? There is not one among you, who could bear to be thought ungrateful. Will you therefore show more unpardonable ingratitude to your Creator, than you *can* to any relation or earthly benefactor ?

6. You all know, that as you become familiar with any object, however beautiful, or striking it may be, you cease to consider it as a matter of in-

terest and importance. You could all crowd to
see an exhibition of artificial fire-works, while
you scarcely think of the sun—the most glorious
of all fire works,—at least as an object of curiosity.

7. Now if we love our country, we must respect the name of the Deity, for the profane man
can never recognise the sanctity of an oath, for
the same reason that you do not feel admiration
and astonishment at the sight of the sun. Then
if oaths be not binding, we will have no means
of eliciting truth in our courts of justice, or of
binding men to a performance of duty, in offices
of high importance.

8. Besides all these considerations, God has
given an express command, "Swear not at all."
We have religion, honor, gratitude and patriotism, and *God himself*, all forbidding profanity.

Questions.—1. What is the subject of this lesson ? 2. What
is it to swear ? 3. Is it a very foolish habit ? 4. Is it polite to
swear ? 5. Is it very wicked ? 6. What is said about profane
swearers in the Bible ?

meant	with-out	there-of	an-oth-er
guilt	pro-found	great-est	ex-cel-lent
dear	feel-ings	re-gard	char-ac-ter
friend	there-fore	man-ners	rel-a-tive

un-grate-ful	ad-mi-ra-tion	for-bid-ding
ben-e-fac-tor	per-form-ance	as-ton-ish-ment
suf-fi-cient-ly	con-sid-er-a-tion	cu-ri-os-i-ty
dis-re-spect-ful	im-por-tance	re-cog-nise

THE

ECLECTIC THIRD READER;

CONTAINING

SELECTIONS IN PROSE AND POETRY,

FROM THE BEST

AMERICAN AND ENGLISH WRITERS.

WITH

PLAIN RULES FOR READING

AND

DIRECTIONS FOR AVOIDING COMMON ERRORS.

BY WILLIAM H. M'GUFFEY,

PRESIDENT OF CINCINNATI COLLEGE—LATE PROFESSOR IN
MIAMI UNIVERSITY, OXFORD.

CINCINNATI:

PUBLISHED BY TRUMAN AND SMITH.

1837.

CONTENTS.

CONTENTS.

POETRY.

LESSON XIX.

More about the Bible.

RULE.—As we cannot read well what we do not understa
we need to study what seems difficult, and look in a Diction
for the pronunciation of all hard words. But it is the *connexion a*
that can give the *true meaning* of words as they are found i
sentence.

1. The *Design of the Bible* is evidently to give
correct information concerning the creation of
things, by the omnipotent word of God; to ma
known to us the state of holiness and happiness
our first parents in paradise, and their dreadful
from that condition by transgression against Go
which is the original cause of all our sin and misery.

2. It is also designed to show us the duty we o
to him, who is our almighty Creator, our bountiful Be
efactor, and our righteous Judge; the method by whi
we can secure his eternal friendship, and be prepar
for the possession of everlasting mansions in his glo
ous kingdom.

3. The Scriptures are especially designed to make
wise unto salvation through faith in Christ Jesus;
reveal to us the mercy of the Lord in him; to fo
our minds after the likeness of God our Savior;
build up our souls in wisdom and faith, in love and ho
ness; to make us thoroughly furnished unto go
works, enabling us to glorify God on earth; and,
lead us to an imperishable inheritance among the sp
its of just men made perfect, and finally to be glorifi
with Christ in heaven.

4. If such be the design of the Bible, how necessa
must it be for every one to pay a serious and prep
attention to what it reveals. The word of God i
vites our attentive and prayerful regards in terms t
most engaging and persuasive. It closes its gracio
appeals by proclaiming, "Whosoever will, let hi
take the water of life freely." The infinite tenderne
of the divine compassion to sinners, flows in the la
guage of the inspired writers, with which they addre

e children of men, and the most gracious promises of
e Lord of glory accompany the divine invitation.

5. We have the most ample and satisfactory proofs
hat the books of the Bible are *Authentic* and *Genuine*;
hat is, that they were written by the persons to whom
hey are ascribed. The scriptures of the Old Testament were collected and completed under the scrupu-
ous care of inspired apostles. The singular provi-
ence of God is evident in the translation of the Old
'estament into Greek, nearly three hundred years be-
ore the birth of Christ, for the benefit of the Jews
who were living in countries where that language was
used.

6. The testimony which our Savior bore to the Old
'estament used by the Jews in Judea, and the quota-
ons which the New Testament writers have made
om its several books, generally from the Greek trans-
ation, confirm what has been already said on the anti-
uity of the Bible, and prove its authenticity.

7. This will appear in a much stronger point of view
when we consider the Jews as the keepers of the Old
'estament. It was their own sacred volume, which
ontained the most extraordinary predictions concern-
ng the infidelity of their nation, and the rise, progress,
nd extensive prevalence of christianity.

8. That all the books which convey to us the history
of the events of the New Testament, were written
nd immediately published, by persons living at the
ime of the occurrence of the things mentioned, and
whose names they bear, is most fully proved. 1. By
n unbroken series of Christian authors, reaching from
he days of the apostles down to the present time.
. By the concurrent and well-informed belief of all
enominations of Christians. 3. By the acknowledg-
ment of the most learned and intelligent enemies of
hristianity.

9. That the books we possess under the titles of
Matthew, Mark, Luke and John, were written by the
persons whose names they bear, cannot be doubted by
ny well-informed and candid mind; because, from the
ime of their first publication, they have been uniformly
ttributed to them by all Christian writers. That all

the facts related in these writings, and all the accoun
given of our Savior's actions and sayings are strict
true, we have the most substantial grounds for belie
ing.

10. Matthew and John were two of our Lord
apostles; his constant attendants throughout the who
of his ministry; eye-witnesses of the facts, and ea
witnesses of the discourses which they relate. Ma
and Luke were not of the twelve apostles; but the
were contemporaries and associates with the apostle
and living in habits of friendship and intercourse wi
those who had been present at the transactions whi
they record.

11. As to the preservation of the sacred books dow
to our times, it is certain, that although the origin
copies may have been lost, the books of the New Te
tament have been preserved without any material a
teration, much less corruption; and that they are, in a
essential matters, the same as when they came from th
hands of their authors. In taking copies of these bool
by writing, from time to time, as the art of printin
was then unknown, some letters, syllables, or eve
words, may have been omitted, altered, or even chan
ed in some manuscripts: but no important doctrin
precept or passage of history, has been designedly
fraudulently corrupted.

12. This would have been impossible: because, a
soon as the original writings were published, gre
numbers of copies were immediately taken, carried b
the evangelical missionaries wherever they went, an
sent to the different churches: they were soon tran
lated into foreign languages, and conveyed into th
most distant countries; they were constantly read i
the Christian assemblies, diligently perused by man
private Christians, some of whom had whole books b
heart. They were quoted by numerous writers, an
appealed to, as the inspired standard of doctrine, b
various sects, who differed from each other on son
important points; and, consequently, they were jea
ously watchful against the least attempt, either to falsif
or to alter the word of divine revelation.

13. The manuscripts of the sacred books are found in every ancient library in all parts of the Christian world; and amount in number to several thousands. About five hundred have been actually examined and compared by learned men with extraordinary care. Many of them were evidently transcribed as early as the eighth, seventh, sixth, and even the fourth centuries.

14. Thus we are carried up to very near the times of the apostles, and the first promulgation of the inspired writings. The prodigious number of these manuscripts, the remote countries whence they have been collected, and the identity of their contents with the quotations which the fathers of different ages have made, demonstrate the authenticity of the New Testament. It has been, indeed, asserted by learned men, that if the New Testament were lost, its contents might be wholly supplied by the quotations from it, which are found in the writings of the fathers of the first four centuries of the Christian church.

————

QUESTIONS.—1. What is the evident design of the Bible? 2. Have we proofs of the authenticity of the Bible? 3. When was the Old Testament translated into Greek? 4. For whose immediate benefit was the translation made? 5. What is confirmed by the quotations of Christ from the Old Testament? 6. How do you prove the authenticity of the New Testament? 7. How could alterations in the Sacred Scriptures have been detected? 8. Where are ancient manuscripts of the Bible now to be found? 9. Do you a think a person could now alter the Bible without being detected? 10. If God has condescended to give us his Word to guide us in the way of eternal life, do you not think that he would extend his protective hand for its preservation?

ERRORS.—*Glo-rous* for glo-ri-ous; *sper-ets* for spir-its; *vol-lum* or vol-ume; *fust* for first; *a-pos-sles* for a-pos-tles.

SPELL AND DEFINE—1. Omnipotent; 2. everlasting; 3. salvation; 5. translation; 6. quotation; 7. predictions; 8. acknowledgments, 9. contemporaries; 11. manuscripts; 12. evangelical 3. promulgation; 14. authenticity.

LESSON XXXI.

On Speaking the Truth.—ABBOTT.

RULE.—Too much pains cannot be taken to acquire familiari
with the stops.

1. A little girl once came into the house, and tol
her mother a story about something which seemed ver
improbable.

2. The persons who were sitting in the room with he
mother did not believe the little girl, for they di
not know her character. But the mother replied
once, " I have no doubt that it is true, for I never kne
my daughter to tell a lie." Is there not something n
ble in having such a character as this?

3. Must not that little girl have felt happy in th
consciousness of thus possessing her mother's entir
confidence? Oh, how different must have been he
feelings from those of the child whose word cannot b
believed, and who is regarded by every one with susp
cion? Shame, shame on the child who has not mag
nanimity enough to tell the truth.

4. There are many ways of being guilty of falsehoo
without uttering the lie direct, in words. Whenever
you try to deceive your parents, in doing that whic
you know they disapprove, you do in reality tell a li
Conscience reproves you for falsehood.

5. Once when I was in company, as the plate o
cake was passed around, a little boy who sat by the side
of his mother, took a much larger piece than he knev
she would allow him. She happened, for the moment
to be looking away, and he broke a small piece off, an
covered the rest in his lap with his handkerchie
When his mother looked, she saw the small piece, an
supposed he had taken no more. He intended to de
ceive her. His mother has never found out what h
did.

6. But God saw him at the time. And do you no
think that the boy has already suffered for it? Must h
not feel mean and contemptible, whenever he think
that, merely to get a little bit of cake, he would deceiv

his kind mother? If that little boy had one particle of honorable or generous feeling remaining in his bosom, he would feel reproached and unhappy whenever he thought of his meanness. If he was already dead to shame, it would show that he had by previous deceit acquired such a character.

7. And can any one love or esteem a child who has become so degraded? And can a child, who is neither beloved nor respected, be happy? No! You may depend upon it, that when you see a person guilty of such deceit, he does, in some way or other, even in this world, suffer a severe penalty. A frank and open-hearted child is the only happy child. Deception, however skilfully it may be practised, is disgraceful, and ensures sorrow and contempt.

8. If you would have the approbation of your own conscience, and the approval of friends, never do that which you shall desire to have concealed. Always be open as the day. Be above deceit, and then you will have nothing to fear. There is something delightful in the magnanimity of a perfectly sincere and honest child. No person can look upon such a one without affection. With this, you are sure of friends, and your prospects of earthly usefulness and happiness are bright.

9. But we must not forget that there is a day of most solemn judgment near at hand. When you die, your body will be wrapped in the shroud, and placed in the coffin, and buried in the grave. And there it will remain and moulder in the dust, while the snows of unnumbered winters, and the tempests of unnumbered summers, sha.i rest upon the cold earth which covers you. But your spirit will not be there. Far away beyond the cloudless skies, and blazing suns, and twinkling stars, it will have gone to judgment.

10. How awful must be the scene which will open before you, as you enter the eternal world! You will see the throne of God: how bright, how glorious, will it burst upon your sight! You will see God, the Savior, seated upon that majestic throne. Angels, in number more than can be counted, will fill the universe with their glittering wings, and their rapturous songs. Oh, what a

scene to behold! And then you will stand in the pre
ence of this countless throng, to answer for every thin
you have done while you lived.

11. Every action and every thought of your life wi
then be fresh in your mind. You know it is written i
the Bible, "God will bring every work into judgmen
with every secret thing, whether it be good or whethe
it be evil." How must the child then feel who has bee
guilty of falsehood and deception, and who sees it the
all brought to light! No liar can enter the kingdom c
heaven. Oh, how dreadful must be the confusion an
shame, with which the deceitful child will then be ove
whelmed! The angels will all see your sin and you
disgrace.

12. And do you think they will wish to have a lia
enter heaven, and be associated with them? No! The
will turn from you with disgust. The Savior will loo
upon you in his displeasure. Conscience will rend you
soul. And you must hear the awful sentence, "Depa
from me, into everlasting fire, prepared for the dev
and his angels."

13. Oh, it is a dreadful thing to practice deceit.
will shut you out from heaven. Though you should es
cape detection as long as you live; though you shoul
die, and your falsehood not be discovered, the time wi
soon come when it will be brought to light, and whe
the whole universe—men and angels will be witnesse
of your shame.

QUESTIONS.—1. What is the subject of this Lesson? 2. What di
the little girl do? 3. What did the company think? 4. What did he
mother say of her? 5. How must the little girl have felt when her mo
ther said she could not doubt her word? 6. What did the boy do
7. What is degrading? 8. Should we ever resort to deception?—
9. If we escape detection for falsehood here, when shall we be detected

ERRORS.—*Set-ling* for sit-ting; *dah-ter* for daugh-ter; *diff-run*
for dif-fer-ent; *fur-git* for for-get.

SPELL AND DEFINE—2. character; 3. consciousness; confi
dence; 4. falsehood; 6. contemptible; 7. disgraceful; 8. mag
nanimity; 10. rapturous; 11. deceitful.

LESSON XXI.

Character of Jesus Christ.—Bishop Porteus.

Rule.—In many words the sound of *h* is suppressed where it should be sounded distinctly; and great caution must be used to avoid this fault.

Examples—*harm, heel, head, hot, horse, who,* are pronounced improperly, *arm, eel, ead, ot, orse, oo.*

1. The morality taught by Jesus Christ was purer, sounder, sublimer, and more perfect than had ever before entered into the imagination, or proceeded from the lips of man. And this he delivered in a manner the most striking and impressive; in short, sententious, solemn, important, ponderous rules or maxims; or in familiar, natural, affecting similitudes and parables.

2. He showed also a most consummate knowledge of the human heart, and dragged to light all its artifices, subtleties, and evasions. He discovered every thought as it arose in the mind; he detected every irregular desire before it ripened into action.

3. He manifested, at the same time, the most perfect impartiality. He had no respect of persons. He reproved vice in every station, with the same freedom and boldness, wherever he found it; and he added to the whole, the weight, the irresistible weight, of his own example.

4. He, and he only, of all the sons of men, acted up, in every minute instance, to what he taught; and his life exhibited a perfect portrait of his religion. But what completed the whole was, that he taught as the evangelist expresses it, *with authority,* with the authority of a divine teacher.

5. The ancient philosophers could do nothing more than give good advice to their followers; they had no means of enforcing that advice; but our great lawgiver's precepts are all *divine commands.*

6. He spoke in the name of God: he called himself the Son of God. He spoke in a tone of superiority, and authority, which no one before him had the courage or the right to assume: and finally, he enforced every thing he taught by the most solemn and awful

sanctions, by a promise of eternal felicity to those who obeyed him, and a denunciation of the most tremendous punishments to those who rejected him.

7. These were the circumstances which gave our blessed Lord the authority with which he spake. No wonder then, that the people 'were astonished at his doctrines,' and that they all declared 'he spake as never man spake.'

———

QUESTIONS.—1. Whose character is here portrayed? 2. What was the character of his instructions? 3. How did the life of Christ correspond with his teachings? 4. Wherein did he differ from the ancient philosophers?

ERRORS.—*Per-fict* for per-fect; *ir-reg-lur* for ir-reg-u-lar; *espress-es* for ex-press-es; *flos-phers* for phi-los-o-phers.

SPELL AND DEFINE—1. morality; sententious; 2. consummate; irresistible; 6. denunciation; 7. doctrines.

THE

ECLECTIC FOURTH READER:

CONTAINING

ELEGANT EXTRACTS IN PROSE AND POETRY,

FROM THE BEST

AMERICAN AND ENGLISH WRITERS.

WITH

COPIOUS RULES FOR READING,

AND

DIRECTIONS FOR AVOIDING COMMON ERRORS.

BY WILLIAM H. McGUFFEY,

PRESIDENT OF CINCINNATI COLLEGE—LATE PROFESSOR IN
MIAMI UNIVERSITY, OXFORD.

Enlarged, Improved, and Stereotyped.

SIXTH EDITION.

CINCINNATI:

PUBLISHED BY TRUMAN AND SMITH.

1838.

CONTENTS.

PROSE.

CONTENTS.

POETRY

LESSON LI.

RULE.—Where two or more consonants come together, let the pupil be careful to sound every one distinctly.

EXERCISES UNDER THE RULE.

It *exists* every where.
Thou *smoothed'st* his rugged path.
Thou *sat'st* upon thy *throne*.
Do you see the *bird's nests?*
Thou *call'st* in vain.
Alkaline *earths*.

Religion the only Basis of Society.

1. Religion is a social concern; for it operates powerfully on society, contributing, in various ways, to its stability and prosperity. Religion is not merely a private affair; the community is deeply interested in its diffusion; for it is the best support of the virtues and principles, on which the social order rests. Pure and undefiled religion is, to do good; and it follows, very plainly, that, if God be the Author and Friend of society, then, the recognition of him must force all social duty, and enlightened piety must give its whole strength to public order.

2. Few men suspect, perhaps no man comprehends, the extent of the support given by religion to every virtue. No man, perhaps, is aware, how much our moral and social sentiments are fed from this fountain; how powerless conscience would become, without the belief of a God; how palsied would be human benevolence; were there not the sense of a higher benevolence to quicken and sustain it; how suddenly the whole social fabric would quake, and with what a fearful crash it would sink into hopeless ruin, were the ideas of a supreme Being, of accountableness, and of a future life, to be utterly erased from every mind.

3. And, let men thoroughly believe that they are the work and sport of chance; that no superior intelligence concerns itself with human affairs; that all their improvements perish forever at death; that the weak have no guardian, and the injured no avenger; that there is no recompense for sacrifices to uprightness and the public good; that an oath is unheard in heaven;

that secret crimes have no witness but the perpetrator; that human existence has no purpose, and human virtue no unfailing friend; that this brief life is every thing to us, and death is total, everlasting extinction; once let them *thoroughly* abandon religion; and who can conceive or describe the extent of the desolation which would follow!

4. We hope, perhaps, that human laws and natural sympathy would hold society together. As reasonably might we believe, that were the sun quenched in the heavens, *our* torches would illuminate, and *our* fires quicken and fertilize the creation. What is there in human nature to awaken respect and tenderness, if man is the unprotected insect of a day? And what is he more; if atheism be true?

5. Erase all thought and fear of God from a community, and selfishness and sensuality would absorb the whole man. Appetite, knowing no restraint, and suffering, having no solace or hope, would trample in scorn on the restraints of human laws. Virtue, duty, principle, would be mocked and spurned as unmeaning sounds. A sordid self-interest would supplant every other feeling; and man would become, in fact, what the theory of atheism declares him to be,—*a companion for brutes.*

————

QUESTIONS.—1. What is the operation of religion upon society? 2. What would be the effect of the removal of religion, upon the whole fabric of virtue? 3. Why would not human laws and sympathies hold society together?

ERRORS.—*vir-too* for vir-tue; *reas'-na-bly* for rea-son-a-bly; *room'-nate* for ru-mi-nate.

SPELL AND DEFINE.—1. contributing, community, diffusing, recognition, enlightened; 2. comprehends, sentiments, powerless, conscience, accountableness; 3. intelligence, recompense, perpetrator; 4. illuminate, unprotected; 5. selfishness, atheism.

LESSON LII.

RULE.—Be careful not to join the last part of one word to the beginning of the next word.

The Steam Boat on Trial.—ABBOTT.

1. The Bible every where conveys the idea that this life is not our home, but a state of probation, that is, of *trial and discipline*, which is intended to prepare us for another. In order that all, even the youngest of my readers, may understand what is meant by this, I shall illustrate it by some familiar examples, drawn from the actual business of life.

2. When a large steamboat is built, with the intention of having her employed upon the waters of a great river, she must be *proved* before put to service. Before trial, it is somewhat doubtful whether she will succeed. In the first place, it is not absolutely certain whether her machinery will work at all. There may be some flaw in the iron, or an imperfection in some part of the workmanship, which will prevent the motion of her wheels. Or if this is not the case, the power of the machinery may not be sufficient to propel her through the water, with such force as to overcome the current; or she may, when brought to encounter the rapids at some narrow passage in the stream, not be able to force her way against their resistance.

3. The engineer, therefore, resolves to try her in all these respects, that her security and her power may be properly *proved* before she is intrusted with her valuable cargo of human lives. He cautiously builds a fire under her boiler; he watches with eager interest the rising of the steam-gage, and scrutinizes every part of the machinery, as it gradually comes under the control of the tremendous power, which he is apprehensively applying.

4. With what interest does he observe the first stroke of the ponderous piston!—and when, at length, the fastenings of the boat are let go, and the motion is communicated to the wheels, and the mighty mass slowly moves away from the wharf, how deep and eager an interest does he feel in all her movements, and in every indication he can discover of her future success!

5. The engine, however, works imperfectly, as every one must on its first trial; and the object in this experiment is

not to gratify idle curiosity, by seeing that she will move, but to discover and remedy every little imperfection, and to remove every obstacle which prevents more entire success. For this purpose, you will see our engineer examining, most minutely and most attentively, every part of her complicated machinery. The crowd on the wharf may be simply gazing on her majestic progress, as she moves off from the shore, but the engineer is within, looking with faithful examination into all the minutiæ of the motion.

6. He scrutinizes the action of every lever and the friction of every joint; here he oils a bearing, there he tightens a nut; one part of the machinery has too much play, and he confines it—another too much friction, and he loosens it; now he stops the engine, now reverses her motion, and again sends the boat forward in her course. He discovers, perhaps, some great improvement of which she is susceptible, and when he returns to the wharf and has extinguished her fire, he orders from the machine-shop the necessary alteration.

7. The next day he puts his boat to the trial again, and she glides over the water more smoothly and swiftly than before. The jar which he had noticed is gone, and the friction reduced; the beams play more smoothly, and the alteration which he has made produces a more equable motion in the shaft, or gives greater effect to the stroke of the paddles upon the water.

8. When at length her motion is such as to satisfy him, upon the smooth surface of the river, he turns her course, we will imagine, toward the rapids, to see how she will sustain a greater trial. As he increases her steam, to give her power to overcome the new force with which she has to contend, he watches, with eager interest, her boiler, inspects the gage and the safety-valves, and, from her movements under the increased pressure of her steam, he receives suggestions for further improvements, or for precautions which will insure greater safety.

9. These he executes, and thus he perhaps goes on for many days, or even weeks, trying and examining, for the purpose of improvement, every working of that mighty power, to which he knows hundreds of lives are soon to be intrusted. This now is probation—*trial for the sake of improvement*. And what are its results? Why, after this course has been thoroughly and faithfully pursued, this floating palace receives upon her broad deck, and in her carpeted and curtained cabins, her four or five hundred passengers, who pour along, in one long procession of happy groups, over the bridge of planks;—father and son—mother and

children—young husband and wife—all with implicit confidence, trusting themselves and their dearest interests to her power.

10. See her as she sails away—how beautiful and yet how powerful are all her motions! That beam glides up and down gently and smoothly in its grooves, and yet gentle as it seems, hundreds of horses could not hold it still; there is no apparent violence, but every movement is with irresistible power. How graceful is her form, and yet how mighty is the momentum with which she presses on her way.

11. Loaded with life, and herself the very symbol of life and power, she seems something ethereal—unreal, which, ere we look again, will have vanished away. And though she has within her bosom a furnace glowing with furious fires, and a reservoir of death—the elements of most dreadful ruin and conflagration—of destruction the most complete, and agony the most unutterable; and though her strength is equal to the united energy of two thousand men, she restrains it all.

12. She was constructed by genius, and has been *tried* and improved by fidelity and skill; and one man governs and controls her, stops her and sets her in motion, turns her this way and that, as easily and certainly as the child guides the gentle lamb. She walks over the hundred and sixty miles of her route without rest and without fatigue; and the passengers, who have slept in safety in their berths, with destruction by water without, and by fire within. defended only by a plank from the one, and by a sheet of copper from the other, land at the appointed time in safety.

13. My reader, you have within you susceptibilities and powers, of which you have little present conception, energies, which are hereafter to operate in producing fullness of enjoyment or horrors of suffering, of which you now can form scarcely a conjecture. You are now on *trial*. God wishes you to prepare yourself for safe and happy action. He wishes you to look within, to examine the complicated movements of your hearts to detect what is wrong, to modify what needs change and to rectify every irregular motion.

14. You go out to try your moral powers upon the stream of active life, and then return to retirement, to improve what is right and remedy what is wrong. Renewed opportunities of moral practice are given you, that you may go on from strength to strength, until every part of that complicated moral machinery, of which the human heart consists, will work as it ought to work, and is prepared to accomplish the

mighty purposes for which your powers are designed. You are *on trial—on probation* now. You will enter upon *active service* in another world.

QUESTIONS.—1. How does the Bible consider this life? 2. What is a state of probation? 3. What is a steam boat? 4. Who invented it? 5. Was Robert Fulton an American? 6. What is meant by proving a steam boat? 7. What is the use of doing it? 8. Is there any resemblance between man and a steam boat? 9. If this life is our state of probation, what will a future state of existence be? 10. What difference is there between man's probation before the "fall" and man's probation now?

ERRORS.—*des-cip-line* for dis-ci-pline; *sar-vice* for ser-vice; *bi-ler* for boil-er; *some-at* for some-what; *sar-tin* and *cer-ting* for cer-tain; *nar-rer* for nar-row; *tre-men-du-ous* and *tre-men-di-ous* for tre-men-dous; *in-jine* for en-gine; *ur-reg-u-lar* for ir-reg-u-lar; *hun-derd* for hun-dred.

SPELL AND DEFINE.—1. conveys, probation, discipline, illustrate; 2. machinery. imperfection, workmanship, sufficient; 3. engineer, cautiously, steam-gage, scrutinizes, apprehensively; 4. ponderous, piston; 5. obstacle, minutely, complicated, minutiæ; 6. friction, lever, reverses, bearing, alteration; 7. equable; 8. safety-valve, pressure; 9. implicit; 10. momentum; 11. ethereal, reservoir, conflagration, unutterable; 12. constructed, fatigue; 13. susceptibilities, conception, conjecture, modify, rectify; 14. renewed.

LESSON XXXVII.

RULE.—Be careful to notice every comma and stop, long enough to take breath.

Benevolence of the Supreme Being.—
CHALMERS.

1. It is saying much for the benevolence of God, to say, that a single world, or a single system, is not enough for it—that it must have the spread of a mightier region, on which it may pour forth a tide of exuberancy throughout all its provinces—that, as far as our vision can carry us, it has strewed immensity with the floating receptacles of life, and has stretched over each of them the garniture of such a sky as mantles our own habitation—and that, even from distances which are far beyond the reach of human eye, the songs of gratitude and praise may now be arising to the one God, who sits surrounded by the regards of his great and universal family.

2. Now, it is saying much for the benevolence of God, to say, that it sends forth these wide and distant emanations over the surface of a territory so ample—that the world we inhabit, lying imbedded as it does, amidst so much surrounding greatness, shrinks into a point, that to the universal eye might appear to be almost imperceptible.

3. But does it not add to the power and to the perfection of this universal eye, that at the very moment it is taking a comprehensive survey of the vast, it can fasten a steady and undistracted attention on each minute and separate portion of it; that at the very moment it is looking at all worlds, it can look most pointedly and most intelligently to each of them; that at the very moment it sweeps the field of immensity, it can settle all the earnestness of its regards upon every distinct hand-breadth of that field; that at the very moment at which it embraces the totality of existence, it can send a most thorough and penetrating inspection into each of its details, and into every one of its endless diversities?

4. You cannot fail to perceive how much this adds to the power of the all-seeing eye. Tell me, then, if it do not add as much perfection to the benevolence of God, that while it is expatiating over the vast field of created things, there is not one portion of the field overlooked by it; that while it scatters blessings over the whole of an infinite range, it causes them to descend in a shower of plenty on every separate habitation; that while his arm is underneath and round about all worlds, he enters within the precincts of every one of them, and gives a care and a tenderness to each individual of their teeming population.

5. Oh! does not the God, who is said to be love, shed over this attribute of his, its finest illustration! when, while he sits in the highest heaven, and pours out his fulness on the whole subordinate domain of nature and of providence, he bows a pitying regard on the very humblest of his children, and sends his reviving spirit into every heart, and cheers by his presence every home, and provides for the wants of every family, and watches every sick bed, and listens to the complaints of every sufferer; and while, by his wondrous mind,

the weight of universal government is borne, oh! is it not more wondrous and more excellent still, that he feels for every sorrow, and has an ear open to every prayer!

———

QUESTIONS.—1. Compared with the whole universe, what is this single world? 2. What must be then, the benevolence which could create such an universe? 3. What higher idea of the intellectual power, as well as goodness of the Creator, does it excite, to reflect, that not the smallest field of this unmeasurable universe, is left unnoticed, or unprovided for? 4. Where is it said that "God is love?"

ERRORS.—*sys-tum* for sys-tem; *ek-zoo-bur-un-cy* for ex-u-ber-an-cy; *hez* and *hed* for has and had; *air* for are; *im-pre-cep-ti-ble* for im-per-cep-ti-ble; *say-in* for say-ing; *set* for sit; *chil-dern* for chil-dren.

SPELL AND DEFINE.—1. mightier, exuberancy, immensity, receptacles, garniture, surrounded; 2. emanations, imbedded, surrounding, imperceptible; 3. comprehension, undistracted, pointedly, intelligently, earnestness, totality, penetrating, inspection, diversities, expatiating, overlooked, teeming, population, subordinate, government; 4. infinite; 5. illustration.

LESSON LIX.

RULE.—Be careful to read the last words of every sentence in as full and loud a tone as the first part.

The Bible.—GRIMKE.

1. The Bible is the only book, which God has ever sent, the only one he ever will send, into this world. All other books are frail and transient as time, since they are only the registers of time; but the Bible is durable as eternity, for its pages contain the records of eternity.

2. All other books are weak and imperfect, like their author, man; but the Bible is a transcript of infinite power and perfection. Every other volume is limited in its usefulness and influence; but the Bible came forth conquering and to conquer: rejoicing as a giant to run his course, and like the sun, "there is nothing hid from the heat thereof."

3. The Bible only, of all the myriads of books the world has seen, is equally important and interesting to all mankind. Its tidings, whether of peace or of wo, are the same to the poor, the ignorant, and the weak, as to the rich, the wise, and the powerful.

4. Among the most remarkable of its attributes, is justice; for it looks with impartial eyes on kings and on slaves, on the hero and the soldier, on philosophers and peasants, on the eloquent and the dumb. From all, it exacts the same obedience to its commandments, and promises to the good, the fruits of his labors; to the evil, the reward of his hands. Nor are the purity and holiness, the wisdom, benevolence and truth of the Scriptures, less conspicuous, than their justice.

5. In sublimity and beauty, in the descriptive and pathetic, in dignity and simplicity of narrative, in power and comprehensiveness, depth and variety of thought, in purity and elevation of sentiment, the most enthusiastic admirers of the heathen classics have conceded their inferiority to the Scriptures.

6. The Bible, indeed, is the only universal classic, the classic of all mankind, of every age and country, of time and eternity, more humble and simple than the primer of the child, more grand and magnificent than

the epic and the oration, the ode and the drama, when genius, with his chariot of fire, and his horses of fire, ascends in whirlwind, into the heaven of his own invention. It is the best classic the world has ever seen, the noblest that has ever honored and dignified the language of mortals!

7. If you boast that the Aristotles and the Platos and the Tullies, of the classic ages, "dipped their pens in intellect," the sacred authors dipped theirs in inspiration. If those were the "secretaries of nature," these were the secretaries of the very Author of nature.

8. If Greece and Rome have gathered into their cabinet of curiosities, the pearls of heathen poetry and eloquence, the diamonds of Pagan history and philosophy, God himself has treasured up in the Scriptures, the poetry and eloquence, the philosophy and history of sacred lawgivers, of prophets and apostles, of saints, evangelists and martyrs. In vain may you seek for the pure and simple light of universal truth in the Augustan ages of antiquity. In the Bible only is the poet's wish fulfilled,

"And like the sun, be all one boundless eye."

QUESTIONS.—1. What does the word Bible mean? 2. How did the Bible come into the world? 3. Did God write the Bible? 4. If men wrote it, how can it be called God's book? 5. Was every part of the Bible written at the same time? 6. What is meant when it is said that the Bible contains the "records of eternity?" 7. How can you show it to be so? 8. Mention six particulars in which the Bible differs from all other books?

ERRORS.—*un-ly* for on-ly; *in-fin-nite* for in-fi-nite; *vol-um* for vol-ume; *in-floonce* for in-flu-ence; *in-trest-in* for in-ter-est-ing; *ph'los-o-phers* for phi-los-o-phers; *con-spic-oo-ous* for con-spic-u-ous; *lan-guidge* for lan-guage; *cu-ros'-ties* for cu-ri-os-i-ties; *re-cords* for rec-ords; *trans-cript* for tran-script; *ti-dins* for ti-dings.

SPELL AND DEFINE.—1. transient, record, eternity; 2. transcript; 4. conspicuous; 5. comprehensiveness, enthusiastic, inferiority; 6. magnificent, classic; 8. curiosities, evangelists, martyrs.

APPENDIX

McGuffey on Education

With the exceptions of his letters, two handwritten sermons, and his book on mental philosophy, all the known writings of William H. McGuffey are listed below. Arranged in order of publication, they include:

1. "Remarks on the Study of the Classics." *Transactions of Fourth Western Institute and College for Professional Teachers*. Cincinnati: Executive Committee, 1834, pp. 203-8.
2. "Contributions to the *Western Monthly Magazine*" (1834). Mimeographed. Oxford, Ohio: McGuffey Museum, Miami University. Including: "General Education," "Reverie," "James Kirkwood," "Seth Bushnell."
3. "Lecture on the Relative Duties of Parents and Teachers." *Transactions of Fifth Western Institute and College for Professional Teachers*. Cincinnati: Executive Commission, 1835, pp. 129-51.
4. "Report on the Most Efficient Methods of Conduct-

ing Exams in Common School High Schools and Academies." *Transactions of Sixth Western Institute and College for Professional Teachers.* Edited by D. C. Talbott. Cincinnati: Executive Commission, 1836, pp. 239-43.

5. "Conversation in a Classroom." *Monthly Chronicle of Interesting and Useful Knowledge,* March, 1839, pp. 147-49.

All but the last item was written before the publication of his Readers.

Other writings of McGuffey include:

1. Oxford, Ohio: Special Collections Library, Miami University. McGuffey letters: A collection written by and to W. H. McGuffey.
2. Oxford, Ohio. Special Collections Library, Miami University. McGuffey sermons: A collection of two handwritten sermons.
3. Oxford, Ohio. Special Collections Library, Miami University. "Mental Philosophy" [unfinished manuscript by W. H. McGuffey]. 3 vols.

The content of his most important essays on education follow.

General Education

This subject can never become trite while properly discussed. No thought is more true, and no truth more important, than that general intelligence is the only palladium of our free institutions. The people are the sovereign—they are more—they are the whole government, both sovereign and subject. They will not err in design, but they may in judgment. Nay, this last is inevitable, unless they possess information adequate to direct them in the functions which they are called to perform. No integrity of principle, no singleness of purpose, no rectitude of intention, can either prevent or postpone political ruin, where the citizen is ignorant of his duties and his rights, and where the legislator, the judge, and the executive are unacquainted with the principles and obligations of their respective offices. The blind are always liable to miss their way, however sincerely they may desire to walk in the right path.

How then can the community be put in possession of that degree of intelligence, which shall prove sufficient to direct them in their suffrages, and in the discharge of those duties to which the suffrage of his fellow-citizens may chance to call every individual of our commonwealth? It may safely be affirmed, that none of the systems of education hitherto, or now in use, will ever effect this desirable object. They are limited in their operation, and defective in their results. Every man, in our government, has a right to participate in the administration of affairs; and some of every class will, as they have done, successfully prosecute their claims to office, notwithstanding their notorious destitution of the necessary qualifications. Of this we are disposed to complain. But what is their fault? They have a *right* to ask such elevation at the hands of their fellow-citizens. Their want of qualifications is their misfortune, not their fault. It may be more justly charged upon those of superior knowledge, inasmuch as they have not done what they ought to have done, and could have accomplished, in diffusing general intelligence throughout the country.

Let us cease then to complain that ignorant men are our rulers; but let us adopt immediately such measures as shall secure to all that information which is adequate to the correct discharge of the duties to which every individual may find himself called by the voice of his country.

Let adequate information be as extensive, or rather as universal, as the right of our citizens to aspire to the performance of public service.

This is obviously practicable. Every man delights in the acquisition of knowledge; and, in our country, *every citizen*, has, or might have, leisure sufficient, without encroaching materially on the time allotted to other pursuits, or required for the maintenance of himself and those dependent on him, to make him a thorough scholar in every branch of practical knowledge immediately pertaining to his duties as a citizen. The leisure enjoyed by our merchants, mechanics, and farmers, is actually greater than that which is at the disposal of professional men. Their general acquisitions, therefore, might be greater.

Let it not be said that the professions of law, medicine, and theology, are in themselves more favorable to mental culture than the pursuits of what are called the laboring classes. If this be true in any respect, it is only because the elementary education of the former has been more favorable to habits of thought and literary pursuits in after life. Let but the early education of the laboring classes be equal to that generally enjoyed by men seeking employment in the learned professions; and the advantages will, in subsequent life, be altogether on the side of those engaged in active pursuits. We have said that they have more leisure than professional men. This needs no other proof than observation. The farmer, the mechanic, and even the merchant, are seen to be less busy men than the lawyer, the doctor, and the divine. It is true, that the first mentioned *may* employ their whole time, and put in requisition all their faculties, in their respective callings. But the professional men of our country, *must* employ their whole time, and devote their undivided energies to the practice of their professions, or they will fail of success, and, what is more, fail in the discharge of their duties. The labors of professional men are, moreover, the labors of the mind; so that, in their short intervals of relaxation, they come to the acquisition of unprofessional, general knowledge, with jaded faculties and relaxed frames—a condition very unfavorable for rapid improvement. Hence, you will see such men seeking, and consistently seeking, relaxation in some active amusement, that will at once relieve the mind and invigorate the body. On the other hand, men engaged in active pursuits, resort to amusements which require but little muscular effort, while they employ agreeably the faculties of the mind. Not only therefore is their leisure greater, but their circumstances are more favorable for employing it to advantage in mental acquisitions.

Their health is usually better; their heads clearer; their minds freer from care; and their time more entirely at their own disposal. This is emphatically the case, at least, with the farmer.

Professional men find more difficulty than perhaps any other class of citizens, in commanding, by their labors, a decent competency for themselves and their families. Hence, embarrassments often prevent that quiet of mind which is indispensable to the acquisition of knowledge. The day-laborer, all things considered, is better paid, and can, upon his seemingly scanty wages, better support that style of life which is expected, or, we may say, demanded of him, than can the president of the United States, with his thousands a year. And so it is, down to the lowest salaried office in the nation. The rules of society require that the style of living be always in proportion to the means supposed to be possessed; and every man in the profession must maintain an apparent equality with the most successful of the corps.

This is much less the case with those who are not employed in public avocations. They may live as they list. They may devote their time as is most convenient or agreeable, without feeling the interference or control of public opinion.

Let but the point of honor be changed, and instead of homage being done to Mammon, let Minerva become the ascendant deity, and the tables will be turned in regard to the comparative intelligence of the two classes. Let but the youth of our country, in general, have such a *common school* education as shall apprise them of their powers; form habits of study and observation; put them in possession of the facts and principles necessary to further improvement; and their intervals of leisure will be transferred from trifling amusements to useful pursuits, from vicious indulgences to the cultivation of the pleasures of taste; and from seeking out methods by which to degrade those that are above them, to the honorable rivalry of attempting to excel them in every species of cultivated excellence. If any thing more be wanting to secure to the laboring classes, at least, an equality in the advantages of an extended education, it would seem to be the correction of an error common to them and a great part of even the educated. It has too long been an almost universal opinion, that the acquisition of scientific knowledge was a thing entirely incompatible with the ordinary or even professional duties of life. Four, five, six, or a dozen years must be spent in elementary and professional studies, during which the student must be employed *exclusively* in the acquisition of knowledge, to the utter neglect of every relative duty; to the abandonment, for the time, of every social enjoyment; to the foregoing of all the sympathies of life; and, in too many instances, to the utter prostration of his physical energies. The stores of knowledge thus acquired, have been generally supposed amply sufficient for all subsequent emergencies. The *graduate* might now sell his text books, abandon his study, and plunging at once into the active duties of life, bid adieu, and forever, to the groves of Academus, without in the least endangering his future celebrity! Nothing can be more preposterous than such an idea. No man ever became eminent from such a course of conduct. Well may it be said, that their educations have been of but little benefit to men who have thus abandoned them at the very crisis when only they could begin to prove advantageous. No wonder that others, without such an early education as might serve to lull them to indolent repose, have, by sedulously improving every moment of leisure, far surpassed their more favored competitors in the race of honor and usefulness. It was not the want of education, on the one hand, but industry, prompted by a sense of that want, which secured success. Nor was it, on the other, the fault of an education, but of the indolence which it occasioned, that disappointment succeeded the brightest hopes.

No man, who does not employ a part of every day of his life in systematic study, need hope for eminence, or even respectability, in literary society, whatever may have been his early education. Nor need any man, of ordinary good sense, despair of distinguishing himself in his own age, and of leaving behind him some monument for posterity, who will but uniformly devote from two to three hours each day to the acquisition of general knowledge or scientific information on a given subject, though his early education may have been totally neglected. Is this theory? Or is it the voice of sober experience?

Look, on the other hand, at Ferguson, and Franklin, and Davy, and Henry, and Clay, and many others, both living and dead, who, without early education, and in the midst of the most pressing poverty, and the unceasing bustle of public life, have risen to an eminence in literature and science, and indeed in every department of human knowledge. On the other, we could, were it not invidious, point out many who, with every advantage that the others did *not* possess, with equal talents, and not unequal ambition, began their descent from fame at the moment when their friends were applauding their maiden effort, and cherishing the fondest hopes of their future eminence. And why these results, so contrary to what was rationally expected? The one class, aware of their deficiencies, supplied them by their industry in after life; and in so doing, formed habits that remained with them while they remained upon earth. The other, presuming upon the superiority secured by their early advantages, suffered indolence, or pleasure, or perhaps dissipation, to break in upon those habits of patient thought, which were only in a forming state when they left the halls of college, or the office of their professional instructor; and thus their former stores were soon squandered, and with them was lost that which was far more valuable, the ability and inclination vigorously to apply themselves to mental pursuits.

We are deliberately of opinion, that the time now spent by the great mass of our youthful population in common schools, is amply sufficient, if properly employed, for acquiring such an education as would render their subsequent progress both easy and delightful.

We could designate individuals who spent less time in their *abecedarian* than usually falls to the lot of the poorest citizen's most unfavored son, and yet found but little obstacle to their future improvement from a defect of elementary knowledge. But it was their singularly good fortune to have competent and faithful instructors, who knew how to develop the mind, and to what extent each branch required to be pursued, so as to yield the greatest assistance in future efforts.

We repeat, then, let but our common schools be properly managed, and elementary studies properly distributed in reference to the several branches afterwards to be pursued; let the people generally be shown that liberal studies are not incompatible with their pursuits; that their leisure and circumstances are peculiarly favorable to their superiority in knowledge; let their notions in regard to the best method of acquiring accurate, practical information, be corrected; let them be induced to make the calculation how long it will take them, by employing only the time which they can conveniently spare from their regular avocations, to equal the time, *the whole time*, usually spent in the acquisition of what is called a liberal education—and the whole community may be expected to rise in their might, and assert their right to an equality in intelligence, as well as in political privileges. To contribute to this result is the duty and the privilege of every citizen, in his proper sphere. We hail the signs of the times as exceedingly auspicious to such an enterprise. The late conventions of professional teachers and others, in different parts of our common country, cannot fail, by their lectures, circulars, and reports, to bring the subject before the proper tribunal—*the public*— and thus the happiest results may confidently be expected. Let every instructor, and every parent, and every citizen, as he may find opportunity, honestly and audibly express his opinion. "In the multitude of counsellors there is safety."

We need facts; we need the results of experience; we need to know the destitutions of our country in regard to education; and, more than all, we need a revised system of public instruction, and faithful, competent, enthusiastic, and persevering instructors to carry it into complete effect.

Then, and not till then, may we expect to see every department of civil society conducted by competent—and if morality and religion keep pace with intelligence—honest men.

These thoughts have been suggested by a perusal of the circular issued by the "local executive committee of the college of professional teachers at Cincinnati." We hope that every person competent to form an intelligent opinion on the subject, will consider the interrogatories as addressed to themselves personally. We know not whether the answers to such inquiries will embrace all that is necessary; but this we do know, that the best way to acquire information on this, or any other, subject, is to go rightly to work. Necessity may be the mother of invention, but wisdom must ever be the result of experience.

DUTIES OF TEACHERS AND PARENTS

Lecture on the Relative Duties of Teachers and Parents

FELLOW-CITIZENS: The time has gone by in which doubts were entertained by the intelligent, as to the necessity and practicability of *general* education.

Our public servants, and professional men, are educated; and the *people must speedily be educated, that they may, on the one hand, protect their own interests; and, on the other, prevent the suspicions and temptation to which popular ignorance must always expose the better informed portions of the community.*

Our citizens, at large, are less informed on subjects connected with the medical profession, than, perhaps, any

other; and, consequently, it is in that profession that thei
credulity is most extensively abused. But in all th
professions, the suspicions that haunt the public mind, an
the credulity that tempts to public abuse, are alike th
offspring of popular ignorance. Honest men, therefore, c
all ranks, will, for their own sakes, desire and strive t
promote the thorough education of the WHOLE PEOPLE
as the only means of allaying suspicions of fraud on the par
of the public, and removing temptation from the path o
those who serve that public.

The *practicability* of educating the whole community
seems to be less convincingly before the minds of thos
concerned than the necessity of such education. And yet
the proof of this proposition, is both more conclusive an
more abundant. What *has* been done *can* be repeated; an
in no country, under heaven, are there to be found suc
facilities for universal intelligence amongst the citizens, as
in our own favored land. Here, a competency can be
acquired, in the lowest classes, by the well-directed labor o
four or five days in each week; and thus, two-sevenths o
their whole time may be appropriated to intellectual and
moral improvement. That state of society must add largely
to the effects of the curse pronounced upon the rebellion o
our first parents, which requires the poor man to spend
more time in earning his bread, than is fairly compatible
with *piety* and *intelligence*. This enterprise, then, if
earnestly undertaken, *must* be successful. There are in
the community abundant resources, both physical and
moral, for the education of the people—the *whole people*—
to any extent that may be found desirable.

But this cannot be effected without effort, and united
effort. There must be concert between the people and their
legislators; between those who are already educated, and
those who have yet to acquire their education; between the
instructors of youth and the parents of the children.

The object of the present lecture is to point out some of
the respective and *relative duties of teachers and parents;*
in order that they may the more successfully co-operate in

their mutual work of training, to intelligence and virtue, the future citizens of our happy republic.

1st. *There must be an increase of teachers.* Not more than thirty pupils ought ordinarily to be committed to the care of a single instructor, at any one time. This ratio must, when all our youth shall be in the schools, augment the number of teachers beyond that of any other profession, or even mechanical employment, in the whole land.

It is the duty, therefore, of our young men, of liberal education, to fill up the ranks of this most *respectable* (and, we trust, soon to be respected) of all professions, the *profession of teaching.* It is the duty of those already engaged in this profession, resolutely to decline all offers of patronage that would involve the necessity of dividing their attention between a greater number of pupils than they can thoroughly instruct. And, as interest and duty are, in the moral government of God, inseparably connected, those who engage in the business of instruction, with a capable facility, cannot fail of employment, and a competent support.

The other professions are full. We have doctors enough; we have lawyers enough; we have politicians more than enough; and if we have not preachers enough, we have certainly more than are *wanted,* or *well paid!* The last fact is evidence of the first. But in the business of instruction, where is the *professional* teacher, much less an *adequate supply* of *professional* teachers, to be found? This field of enterprise, if not new, is certainly almost unoccupied. No where else can talents, and learning, and worth find such certain and profitable investment.

But if it were even not so, still it would be the duty of teachers to persevere; and of those who are competent to teach, to commence and persevere, until the ranks should be filled up, and the public compelled, by the force of truth and experiment, to award to the faithful and competent instructor of youth, the honor and maintenance which are his due. The work *must* be done. The existence of our institutions depends upon it. The people have been complaining (and they have had cause to complain) that teachers were not worthy of their patronage; and the teachers have, in turn, complained that their compensation was not equal to their toil; and these complaints have been but too lamentably just. But, fellow-teachers, crimination and recrimination will not reform the abuse. Grant that our compensation has not been equal to our pains, is there any better way to liberalize our patrons than by doing our work faithfully, and on more patriotic principles? But, fellow-teachers, we are not to depend upon the mere fee for tuition as even our *pecuniary* reward. Our profession has a rare felicity in this respect—that while others find employment from the miseries and vices of mankind, our gain, both in the extent and profit of the employment which we receive, will be in proportion to our success in diffusing through the community a love of learning and an adherence to sound morals and true religion. The more intelligence is diffused through the community, the more will the desire to improve be increased. And in proportions as the business of instruction is understood, will impossibilities cease to be expected of the instructor. Besides, the effect of correct knowledge, in promoting the general prosperity of society, and in enhacing the value of property already acquired, must secure for the teacher, as a member of the community, an adequate, though sometimes protracted reward for his labor and his time. It is *knowledge* that prompts to enterprise and devises plans for the general good. It is knowledge that renders available facilities for the accumulation of property, and the suppression of expensive crime.

It is knowledge, and morality, the offspring of knowledge that alone can give general prosperity to society, and thus benefit all, and, consequently, the school-master; whose business it is to promote both knowledge and morality, in his official capacity. It is our duty, then, fellow-teachers, and we rejoice to add, our *privilege*, to labor assiduously in our vocation—a vocation which, though it might receive no *direct* reward, must compensate us, by the general prosperity which it cannot but promote, and with the least possible tendency to selfishness, because it is in common with *all* our fellow-citizens.

2d. In the former topic we deduced our interest from our duty; in this let us learn our duty, in the light of our interest. We may know what we ought to do, when we have learned what is rightly expected of us.

The faithful and competent teacher never fails to secure the confidence, respect, and even affection of his pupils. He is as he ought to be, esteemed "in place of a parent." He is thought to be infallible. He *ought* therefore to be correct. He is esteemed as possessing the whole cyclopedia of knowledge. He ought, therefore, to be a man of extensive acquaintance with the principles of science. He is thought by the confiding pupil, to be incapable of any measure, or even intention, at variance with honest views of promoting the best interests of those entrusted to his care. And he ought, accordingly, to enlist all his energies in promoting the solid improvement and moral growth, of every mind submitted to his influence.

Nor does his influence stop here. We go out into the world, and retain our schoolhouse impressions of our former instructor. No matter what may be our mental superiority, or subsequent acquisition; we still think of our former school-master, as the same great man, which relatively to ourselves, he *was* in the period of our novitiate. And from this, fellow-teachers, our duty is clear. We *ought*, as far as possible, to continue through the whole period of our lives, as far in advance of those who were once our pupils, as we were found to be upon their introduction to us. The same *proportion* cannot be preserved—but the same *distance* in advance may. I am not *twice* as old as you, who are more than half my age—but I shall always continue *as many years* older than you, as I was at first. The more we know, the more rapidly can we acquire. Why then is our improvement less in riper years than it was in our youth? Obviously, because our industry has declined; our attention to the business of our profession has become relaxed. The experience of *individuals* alone can increase the knowledge of mankind. He therefore, who is faithful to himself, will while he contributes to the general improvement of the species, by his own accurate observation, be able, by the same means, to avail himself of all the advantage of the general stock of information to which he is a contributer.

Here are two men, equally ardent in their pursuit of useful discoveries. The one has knowledge enough to fit him to become the instructor of the other; and they are about equal in strength and capacity of mind. Which do you suppose, will most likely succeed in making discoveries? The one undoubtedly, (other things being equal,) who has the most knowledge. If we were unacquainted with their relative acquisitions we should feel safe to infer, as a general result, that he who succeeded best, must necessarily know most. "Knowledge is power." And in proportion to the efficiency so will be the effect, wherever that power is applied. Why then should *old men* fall behind the age in which they live? And of all old men, aged teachers are most inexcusable for this, which so frequently happens.

The expectation, then that teachers will continue to improve, is a rational one, nay, almost instinctively rational; and we are bound, therefore, to versify it, by our industry. We, fellow-teachers, must mold the opinion of society, especially on all subjects connected with education, I say *must* because, from the nature of the case we cannot avoid it, if we would. The future opinions, plans, and enterprises of our pupils, on these subjects, will be not only tinged, but characterized, if not created by our influence upon their forming minds. All that they shall hereafter think, will in great measure, be the *results* of what we have previouisly thought, and inculcated. With us rest the tremendous responsibility of laying the *foundation* of a nation's literature; and of saying what shall be its future character, for morality and religion.

The foundation *can* be laid but ONCE. The character of the superstructure, does not depend so much upon those who shall complete the edifice, as upon us, who are called to lay the corner stone. Let us then, divest ourselves of all selfish views; of every narrow prejudice; of every local preference; and of the whole class of temporary expedients, and come up to the work with a zeal, a devotedness, and perseverance worthy of so good a cause. Let us remember too, that when those who are now our pupils, shall have become the legislators and governors of the republic; when they shall have devised means, raised funds, organized colleges, and founded universities, and are looking out for those, to whose care these institutions shall be entrusted, that their attention will most be directed to *us*, their former instructors. This will be both natural and just. All these their doings will, we have said, take their character from our former instructions. Who then, so suitable to carry into effect those principles and plans, as those with whom they have virtually originated? But in order to this,—we must never sleep at our post—we must continue to improve, we must add the experience of yesterday to that of today, and the experience of both to the business of tomorrow.

We must accumulate the experience of the whole profession, in the person of each individual, and personally add to the stock from which we so largely borrow. We must study the human mind; and watch it, in all its varieties of development and growth. We must become *scientific* and not *empirical* teachers, who shall know how to give permanent direction—to the public mind; and not content ourselves with that evanescent or erroneous impression, which disappears of itself, or requires to be effaced, to make room for that which shall be both more correct and more enduring.

If we become dilatory, and cease to improve, we shall be guilty of alternately defeating those very plans, which through our earlier pupils, we have ourselves matured. For, that we shall not be permitted (or be inclined) to retire, is demonstrated by facts—most of our Presidents of colleges have been called to these present places, of honor and trust, by their former pupils—many of the professors, in our literary institutions, have been selected, by intelligent men of other professions, from among those to whom they recited in the *log school-house;* or, the but little more pretending academy. And it will, because it *must* continue to be so. Illy qualified for promotion, as most of our profession may be found to be—still, our experience, in despite of our indolence, gives us a decided advantage over gentlemen of any other profession, in the management of literary institutions. Few instances are on record, of gentlemen taken from the bar, or the pulpit, or the profession of medicine, that have succeeded as the *presidents* of colleges, or universities. And fewer still, are the recorded instances of TEACHING PROFESSORS (for any one may *compile* and *read lectures,*) who have not found their way to the professor's chair through all the grades of elementary instruction, up from the "common school." Let us take special care then, to acquire the skill which shall be requisite to cultivate, in its approaching maturity, that tree of science, which we ourselves are planting; and which if left by us, *must* be abandoned to still less skilful hands.

3d. In the preceding remarks, we have noticed duties that are less relative, than those which remain to be mentioned. But here, as before, we may discover our duty, fellow-teachers, from the trust reposed in us. Parents commit to us their richest treasures, their dearest hopes. In this they are too exclusive; but their fault cannot lessen our responsibility. It rather increases it. We have the formation of *character* committed to us. The intellectual habits of our pupils will be very much as we form them. Their modes of thought—their principles of taste—their habitude of feeling, will all take their complexion, if not their character, from our methods of training the mind. Who then can enter the classroom without trembling? Where is the spirit stout enough to try *experiments* upon an immortal mind? No man is fit to teach who does not understand human nature. Nor will an empirical knowledge of the mind suffice. Principles and experiment must go together. Theory, without practice, will be mischievous; and practice without theory must, of course, be at random.

We owe it, then, to our pupils, and to their parents, thoroughly to understand what we profess to teach. For who can communicate intelligibly to another, that which he himself does not clearly comprehend? That man is a swindler of the worst description, who "procures, upon false pretences," the *intellectual* wealth of the community, and submits to, he cares not what, venturous process, for his own paltry and sordid gain. The fraudulent merchant destroys but the fortunes of those whom he plunders. But the incompetent teacher ruins the immortal mind, which is of more value than all temporal riches.

Nor is it enough *once* to have understood what we profess to teach. We must constantly review our studies. This is necessary in order to promptness of explanation; without which, much time must be lost to our pupils, and sluggish habits of mental action, unavoidably induced upon both us and them. We should be master of our subject—familiar with its details—clear in our explanations—rapid in our mental movements—glowing in our conceptions of truth—impassioned in our endeavors to produce the same results on the minds of our pupils.

But the most difficult part of a teacher's duty, arises from the great variety of intellectual and moral character, found amongst his numerous pupils. No two minds are alike, in all their powers and susceptibilities. Every mind, therefore, requires a mode of treatment, somewhat different from that which is suitable for any other mind; and here, both the skill and the honesty of the teacher are put to the test. Every new pupil is, not only a new *lesson*, but a new book, which the teacher *must* study! And a book too, in which new pages are continually unfolding, which require a new analysis, and frequently compelling a change of estimate, and consequently a change of procedure, in regard to the whole matter. In such cases, fellow-teachers, it is feared, that ability sometimes, and industry much more frequently, may fail. Let us be on our guard here. Let no temptation, of a higher fee, induce us to advance a pupil to higher studies, for which he is not prepared. Let not our indolence prevail with us, to class others with those who are obviously their inferiors in either talents or acquirements, much less in both, that we may thus lighten our own labors, at the expense of their improvement and "mental training." Let not our misjudging desire for popularity or patronage, ever suggest the thought of lowering the standard of education, in our public institutions. Such conduct is not only dishonest, in public teachers, but clearly impolitic. A "short course" can be a recommendation only to short-sighted judges, whether pupils or parents. Those are certainly enemies to the dearest interests of their country, whether intentionally or not, who erect depositories for intellectual *chaff;* scrape together, that which has not substance enough to abide the siftings and winnowings of a thorough education, nor weight enough to find its proper level when separated from the purer mass; manufacture it by some new but patent process, which requires but little time, and less labor, though frequently at great expense to the owners; and then throw it into the market, bearing falsely, the brand of a genuine article, to the defrauding of an unsuspecting public, and the ultimate disparagement of all sound education. Nor can any censure, too severe, be passed upon that instructor, who can, for the sake of popularity, or any such motive, lower the standard, or relax the discipline of a co-ordinate, or subordinate school, or department in a school, connected with our general system.

Let us then be honest with ourselves; honest with our pupils; honest with their parents; and honest with the public. Let us not drive a pupil too fast, and thus destroy the vigor and energy of his mental action. Let us not check the natural activity of his thought; and thus induce a habit of mental *moping*, alike unfriendly to accuracy and despatch, whether in acquisition or execution. Let us not flatter our patrons, that their children are capable of professions, for which nature never intended them. Let us be careful never to inculcate any *doubtful* principle of morality or religion; or to recommend, by precept or example, any wrong, or even equivocal sentiment or feeling.

We may, nay we must, have our own speculative opinions—hypotheses in morals, which we have not yet been able either to verify or disprove by inductive experience. But, in this state, fellow-teachers, let them never once be named in our schools: nor let them begin to influence our conduct as practical teachers. The intellectual and moral character of our pupils is too valuable, to be made the subject of rash and hazardous experiment.

The Christian religion, is the religion of our country. From it are derived our prevalent notions of the character of God, the great moral governor of the universe. On its doctrines are founded the peculiarities of our free institutions. From its sanctions are derived the obligations to veracity imposed in the administration of justice. In its revelations are found the only certain grounds of hope in reference to that, else unknown future, which lies beyond the horizon of time. It alone places a guard over the conscience, which never slumbers, and whose eye cannot be evaded by any address of the delinquent. Its maxims, its precepts, its sentiments, and even its very spirit, have become so incorporated with the mind and soul of civilization, and all refinement, that it cannot be eradicated, or even opposed, without imminent hazard of all that is beautiful, lovely, and valuable in the arts, in science, and in society.

Let us then, fellow-teachers, avoid, on the one hand, the inculcation of all sectarian peculiarities in religion: and on the other, let us beware of incurring the charge, (which will not fail to be made,) of being enemies to our country's quiet, by teaching to our pupils the crude notions, and revolutionary principles of modern infidelity. It is, at best, but an unsustained *hypothesis*.

4. The duties that remain to be noticed, in the fourth place, as incumbent on teachers, in relation to the parents of those who are their pupils, are, if possible, more important than any that have yet been noticed. Teachers ought to know best *how* to do that which is required of them—but parents are, or ought to be, the better judges, as to *what is*

to be done. We, fellow-teachers, are the servants of the public. We have a deep interest, as has been shown, in the results of our own labors in their effects upon public prosperity and national character. But, much as we love, and ought to love those committed to our care, they are but our pupils, not our children. This last relation is one which can be constituted only by the author of our being. All attempts, artificially to form it, must end in comparative defeat. None but the *natural* parent, can feel that natural affection, which is adequate to the duties of *properly educating* an immortal mind.

Our duties, then, paradoxical as it may seem, are only subordinate in that very business which we pursue as a profession. The teacher, I repeat, should know better than any other man, how to produce a given result in mental training; but the parent, who is the natural guardian, or in want of parents, the authorised adviser, alone has the right to say what that result, which is attempted, shall be.

Let us then pursue such a course as shall be most likely to interest parents in the progress, as well as the results of our labors. Let us encourage them to visit our schools; to take part in the examinations of *our* scholars, but *their own* children. Let us refuse those, whose parents will not co-operate with us, or who decline giving a specific view of what they wish us to accomplish, in behalf of their children. Let us, like the mechanic insist upon definite instructions, as to what is to be done; and then, like him, let us throw ourselves upon our skill, and the intelligence of our patrons, for our character, and our reward.

The second general division of our subject, is the duties incumbent on *parents*, in the business of education.

And here, as in the first division of this discourse, I have the pleasure to rank with those whom I address. I have long been a teacher; and expect to remain in the profession for life. But I am also a parent, who has children to educate, and may therefore be supposed to feel, in some degree at least, the importance of those duties which I venture to urge upon my fellow-citizens.

As, in the preceding remarks, the duties of teachers have been shown to be subordinate to those of parents; so, in what is to follow, I wish the paramount importance of the parents interests, and the parent's duties to be kept distinctly before us. We who are parents are the employers—teachers our assistants, in the all reponsible business of training up the future governors of this republic, who are to give character to the world, and to form characters for eternity.

1. In the first place, we must provide suitable accommodations for our schools. Children cannot learn when uncomfortable. And they cannot be comfortable, either in cold weather, or in hot, unless the school-house, or recitation room, be such as can be both warmed and ventilated, as occasion may require. How much time, and money, and that which is more valuable than both time and money, I mean mind, is wasted; simply for the want of suitable buildings for schools? Nor is mere convenience, of itself, sufficient. Children are creatures of association and habit; and much depends upon the cheerfulness and taste of that which is connected with their early mental efforts, as to whether they shall become attached to study, and take a delight in thought; or shall contract a disgust for every thing like literature and science. Time was, when the log school-house, with gable-end chimney, clap-board door, and long, narrow windows, papered and greased, was all that could be looked for, in a country that was still a wilderness. But that time is now past. And yet, even these *cabin colleges* were often more comfortable, and better conducted, than some of our public schools, at the present day. It must make the heart of philanthrophy bleed, to see the youth of our country so frequently collected, (when in school at all,) in uncomfortable, and even filthy hovels, in which the farmers of the neighborhood would hardly consent to house their sheep; surrounded by every thing calculated to disgust them with learning, and to make them loathe even the sight of a slate or a book. But on the other hand, in contact, as if by design, with whatever can minister to

grossness of sentiment, confusion of thought, and ferocity of character. And all this, for want of such accommodations, as could be procured for a less sum than one half of that which those most intimately concerned are known to expend upon that which is worse than useless. I make these remarks with the greater freedom, because they are generally known to be true—and because, from the enterprise of this city [Cincinnati] they cannot be construed as conveying any reproof to those who constitute the present audience. And yet, the newly painted spires of your public school-houses, and other literary edifices, seem to imply, fellow-citizens, that it is but recently, since the spirit of improvement commenced its work, even amongst *you.* But the extent of that work, in so short a time, is the more honorable to the enterprise that has accomplished it.

2. The next duty devolving upon parents, in relation to teachers, is to furnish them with suitable tools, with which to work. They must, we have seen, have comfortable shops—a school-house is the teacher's shop—but this will not avail, unless those shops be furnished. We must furnish or compensate the teachers for furnishing *uniform sets* of suitable class books. No teacher can instruct successfully when the variety of books is nearly equal to the whole number of scholars. Every thing that saves time to the teacher, must benefit the school. And nothing is more desirable to a conscientious instructer, than to be able to devote a large portion of his time to every individual under his care. But this cannot be done without careful classification, which classification is impossible without a uniformity of class books. As we value the improvement of our children, then we ought not only to permit, but to encourage the instructers whom we employ, to introduce as rigid a system of classification, and as great a uniformity of books, into the schools, as possible. But still more than books, and classifying is needed to furnish a school-room. Our teachers must have maps and globes, and a variety of apparatus, suitable to illustrate these branches of knowledge, which we expect our children to learn. But the

compensation which we ordinarily allow them, is not sufficient to warrant, or enable them to procure these articles, at their own cost. *We* must furnish them; and in doing so, we shall be the gainers. Our children will learn more rapidly; understand more clearly what they do learn; and retain with more permanency, and greater accuracy, the principles of those practical sciences, which even a school apparatus is sufficient to illustrate.

3. But, to keep up the figure of a shop—it is not enough that our teachers have tools—they must also have stock, or the raw material upon which these tools are to be employed, and their skill expended. This material, parents are to furnish; and it is of vast importance, to success in the result, that it be of the right kind. Children receive their characters from the preponderant impressions to which they are habitually exposed. Thus their characters will be formed within the domestic circle. Teachers *can* do but little to alter the tendencies of that almost uninterrupted, influence exerted upon young minds by the example of parents, domestics, and friends. Nay, it has before been shown, that it was not the province of the teacher, to oppose, what must be presumed to be the deliberate arrangement of the family circle, in relation to children. Teachers must not only take children as they are; but must permit them to remain as they were, in the respects just noticed. For where is the parent, that will patiently permit any teacher to obliterate those impressions; or change those characteristics; or to interfere with the formation of those habits, in his children, which he has been so solicitous to secure? For I cannot, I will not suppose; that there is a single parent who hears me, that is so ignorant of the facts, or so regardless of the consequences just stated, as not to give all possible attention to the arrangement of every part of his domestic relations, in reference to its influence upon the education, and consequently upon the character of the children belonging to the family.

We, then, who are parents, must from the constitution of society, form and sustain, the character, intellectual and moral, of those who reside under our roof. The teacher cannot do it without our aid; nor ought he to be permitted to do it without our co-operation. We must lay the foundation; he may help us to build. We must furnish the materials; he may fit and adjust them; but only under our direction and supervision. The teacher may, and will exert an incalculable influence upon the minds of his pupils; and through them on society. But parents are responsible for a great part even of that—because it will be modified by their superior, and anticedent influence. The result will be different, and something more than would follow from parental education alone—or else the employment of teachers would be useless. But it never can be much different, in kind or degree, from the general character of that influence, which is exerted by the specific circumstances of the domestic fire-side.

What then is our duty in this business? We shall best answer the question, by ascertaining what are the chief hindrances to success in our own attempts to communicate information to the infant mind. We will not stop to enumerate, much less to classify these hindrances here. We shall take for granted, that they are familiar, and distinctly recognized by all, as they must be, by every parent who has done his duty in the instruction of his family. These we must labor to remove, as much as possible, out of the way of the teacher. We must, as far as practicable, so arrange matters at *home*, that our children may come into the hand of the school-master, docile, ingenuous affectionate, intelligent, honorable, magnanimous, rational, conscientious, and pious children. These are the fundamental elements of a right character; and *not one* of them can be dispensed with, in the very commencement of a school education. Or if there *is one*, which will any father, or mother, in this audience designate to be excluded? Or which one would any parent be willing, were it possible, should spring up in the mind of the child, under the fostering care of any hand but his own? Where is the mother that would not resent the imputation, that her child had grown old enough to attend school, without her having cherished or implanted in its opening mind, one and every one, of the principles above enumerated? I know it was once objected, that *piety* was not compatible with the infant mind. But the author of the only true religion, ever professed by men, was of a different opinion. He recognized in the minds of "little children" something so *like* to piety, in the adult mind, that he made the former a *test* of the genuineness of the latter. "Except ye be converted, and become as *little children*, ye shall not enter into the kingdom of heaven." Piety is right sentiments towards supreme excellence. And would not the parent who should discourage *that*—run an awful risk, of obliterating *all* right sentiments in relation to *every species* of moral excellence? How could he after this, hope to maintain his authority, as a father? Or command the respect of his child?

But it may be said—that these are the traits of an educated mind—and instruction has become useless where these principles exist. It is admitted that education, neither purchased nor domestic, can *implant* such principles—*piety* for example. But some of the above traits are *habits*—and all require to be cherished at first by a *parent's hand*. And if they are not, it will be little less than miraculous should they survive the rude culture and the chilling atmosphere of public instruction, in its best forms. They can be cherished at home. They are successfully cherished in many families. But we might challenge the world, to produce, even a few instances, where they have been successfully cultivated, in any other field.

Let me not be misunderstood. I do not say that *any principle* can be implanted by education. Piety is the result of divine agency; but may be cherished by human means. All I contend for here, is, that the fundamental elements of character cannot be so well, if at all, developed any where else, as in the family; nor by any other hand, so appropriately as by that of a parent. Infant piety, youthful ingenuousness, and juvenile honor, are of too delicate a texture, to bear an early transplanting into our public

schools—even those which are under the best possible
regulations.

Let us then, who are parents, prepare our children for
the school, by training them to *think* by means of *rational
conversation;* by cherishing honesty of character, through a
proper treatment of their natural ingenuousness; by
cultivating in them a respect for all that is valuable, and
praiseworth in human character around them; by teaching
them a *rational* subordination to just authority, as con
nected with intelligence superior to their own, and an
undoubted intention to promote their interest; by encourag
ing them to examine into the grounds of even authoritative
injunctions, not that they may find reasons to disobey, but
that they *may obey more intelligently;* by showing, what
we must be careful honestly to feel, a uniform respect for
those whom we employ, to assist us in the business of
educating those minds, which God has entrusted to our
care—and thus exciting in their minds, that respect and
confidence towards their instructors, which is ever found
indispensable in the business of instruction. How inconsis
tently some parents are found to act in this matter! It is
inconsistent to employ as an instructor a person whom we
cannot respect; and even if this should happen, through
mistake, it is highly injudicious to manifest disrespect
towards their teacher, in the presence of our children, until
we are fully prepared to remove them from his care.
Parents are commendably careful, not to marry their
daughters to unworthy men. But why should we not be
equally careful, not to commit either our sons, or our
daughters, to the care of disreputable teachers? Will it be
said that the former connection is for life; the latter but
temporary? I reply, the influence of the former is upon
happiness only—that of the latter upon *character* first, and
subsequently upon happiness.

We owe it as a duty, to the whole profession of teachers,
to discourage every thing in them that is wrong, by
resolutely refusing to employ, at any price, those who are
not of reputable character; and to encourage whatever is

commendable by showing *equal respect* for virtue and excellence in that profession, as to that in any other. We owe it, moreover, to teachers, and to the public, not to send to an institution of learning, a young man of insubordinate temper, or bad moral character. How often are both teachers, and students in our public seminaries, most grossly imposed upon, by the stealthy introduction of such young men, as never ought to have been admitted into any public institution, unless perhaps it were a penitentiary. Schools and colleges are not houses of correction. They were intended to *educate;* not to *reform* young men. But these are our own sons, and we are anxious to reclaim them. Very well. And so are all our friends, and the public. But this gives us no right to jeopard the morals of others, from the very slight prospect of good to our own unfortunate children. The risk of increasing, or of at least spreading the moral contagion, is much too great to warrant any judicious, much less conscientious man, so to offend against the morals of his country, as to cast poison into the fountains of science. The whole community should unite in reprobating the man who should introduce the *cholera* into an institution of learning, induced by the hope of recovering the patient infected, even though that patient were an only son. But to introduce *a moral pestilence* is still worse than this.

4. The last class of duties, devolving on parents in relation to teachers must be briefly discussed, for the present. It has been frequently hinted, in the progress of the lecture, that the business of instruction was a joint concern, of the teacher and the parent. The part which the parent must take in it, throughout, comes now to be noticed, in its most important aspect. And that is, fellow-citizens, we must *ourselves* be the prominent and persevering teachers of our children, during the whole period, in which their characters are forming. We must subordinate every other concern to that. We must not leave it to hired help. We must not permit either business or pleasure, or even other duties, (none can be paramount,) to interfere with this class of obligations. We must not allow

any man to dictate to us in the course which we pursue; nor must we ever lose sight of the actual engagements which employ our children from day to day.

We must here, as in other business, *superintend* at least, the whole concern, or it will not succeed. Let us decide what our children are to learn—procure for them suitable accommodations, books and apparatus—employ, for their benefit, the ablest instructors—and then keep our eye constantly upon them, their progress, and their instruction—encourage their despondency—repress their waywardness—show an interest in their studies, or we may be assured they will not. In a word, let us post up, *every day*, the whole concern, that we may have it under our eye, and let all concerned know that it is so.

Is it objected, that we have not time, thus to attend to the education of our children, in person. The answer is, we have as much time to spare from business, as our children have from amusement, and healthful exercise. But if time be wanting, then let us employ assistants, in our other avocations. Why should ladies fear to trust the management of household affairs to the exclusive care of servants, while they make no scruple of abandoning the education of their daughters, to those who are not, or are not known to be, any better qualified for their task, than servants are for theirs? Why should fathers consider it indispensable to superintend, in person, the concerns of their farms or their shops, or their merchandise; while they wholly neglect the proceedings of the school, to which are sent those sons for whom they are thus laboring? If we want leisure, let us employ more help, in every department of our business; but let us not be seduced, nor withheld by any engagements, so as not carefully to accompany our children, on the thorny path of elementary acquisition.

But we are ourselves ignorant of many things which we wish our children to learn; and in these we may be excused from accompanying them. If they are valuable acquisitions, and useful in life, (and children should not be doomed to study any thing of a different character,) our ignorance furnishes an additional motive why we should accompany our children in these very studies. We can hardly claim respect for our opinions from those who are confessedly wiser than ourselves. We ought, therefore, in defence of our authority, to keep pace with the improvements in school education. Besides, we can hardly hope that our children will be much interested in those studies, which they are aware we are ignorant of, unless we show sufficient interest to be willing yet to attend to them. If, when they come to us with a difficulty, which they have met with in their lesson, we put them off, with a declaration that either we do not understand, or do not care about what they are studying, can we be surprised, or blame them if they show but little further concern in the matter? But even if it should prove impracticable (which I believe it will do only through indolence) to learn what our children are learning, though we may not have acquired it before, still we can show an interest in their studies like that of the heathen mother, who, though she could not read, yet required her son to read to her his daily lesson at the school, and judged of his proficiency, as she could, by general appearances, so that she correctly applauded his industry and rebuked his indolence, as they respectively occurred. Your speaker has seen the grandfather of eight years, induced to look into geography, in order to correct his little grandson, that glaring heresy of modern times, *that the earth turns round on its axis,* and after pronouncing the assertions of the little philosopher *"nonsense"*—"silly nonsense," became interested in the child's artless defence of his book, and finally to take lessons from his pupil, and become a companion of his studies for months together. The results were valuable. They showed that an aged man, in the midst of business engagements, could learn a new science; and that the effects of such a companionship were most salutary upon the mind of the child. That child was my pupil, and far surpassed his classmates, from the time he took his grandfather into partnership in his studies.

Every intelligent teacher will expect success, just in

proportion as he can induce parents to take an interest in the business which he conducts, but which they must superintend. Let parents then be the instructors of their own children—employing all the assistance they may need or desire; but never *resigning* the business into the hands of another.

It must be obvious, from the foregoing remarks, that children and youth ought to be kept under the parental roof, during the period of their elementary education; and the experience of public teachers abundantly confirms the remark. A very large proportion of those who leave their parental home, before their characters are pretty well confirmed, are more or less injured, and many of them ruined, by their residence at even our most respectable public schools.

How can it be otherwise? Who is to watch over the daily conduct of the stranger student? His instructers cannot do it; and if they are honest men they will not engage to do that which they know is, from the nature of the case, impracticable. The young man is, in a great degree, cut off from the restraints of society, the advice of friends, and the protection of parents. He is exposed to the excitement of a hundred companions, who, like himself, are deprived of the ordinary amusements found in social life, and left to expend that buoyancy of spirit, which even the severest study cannot always suppress, in boisterous mirth, or acts of mischief.

His steps are watched by the unprincipled and designing, who take advantage of the excellencies of his generous nature, to lead him into vice, for their own sordid gain. And often, alas too often, all that remains, after the period of education has elapsed, is the wreck of what was once a noble spirit, but now fallen.

How poor a compensation is a little *knowledge* for the loss of moral excellence? How pitiful the acquisition of mental dexterity, at the expense of all correct habits. Teachers may instruct, but society must *educate*. And what society can be compared with that which is enjoyed around a father's table, and under the domestic roof? No responsibilities are more reluctantly assumed, or more painfully regretted, than those which are imposed upon the officers of literary institutions in the west, by the absurd practice of sending sucklings to college. We must then have schools, within the reach of every family, sufficient to give to the son of every American citizen, an education that shall enable him to discharge the highest duties, to which his fellow citizens may appoint him; and to the daughter of every American mother, such a one as shall fit her to become the wife and mother of freemen.

Fellow-citizens, my thoughts, on this subject, are now before you. The importance of the topics discussed, must be my apology for the length of the lecture. Let teachers fill up the ranks of the profession; let them trust to the inevitable effects of their well directed labors, for their reward; let them be careful to improve as society advances; and let them be content with their subordination to parents, as the only effectual means of bringing every power of society into requisition in the business of universal education.

And, on the other hand, let parents come up to the work as *they* ought. Let them provide suitable houses, suitable books, suitable apparatus, and suitable instructors for the benefit of their children; and all this within reach of their own homes. And let them be careful to cherish in their children those traits of character, that will make them at once active, and docile, respectful and persevering. And, in addition to all this, let them, as they would discharge the high responsibility that heaven has laid upon them, accompany their children through all their studies, and, in person, superintend the whole process of their mental, moral, and religious training. And, through the blessing of Heaven, the result will be as they could wish. "Train up a child in the way he should go, and when he is old, he will not depart from it,"—is a declaration that never *has*, and never *will* be falsified. It is the declaration of ETERNAL TRUTH.

CONVERSATIONS IN A SCHOOL ROOM

No. 1.

Teacher. What is the meaning of the word "*latent*" which occurred in the lesson just read?

First Pupil. I do not know, unless it means *bad*.

T. That would not make sense, in the connexion where it is found. The phrase is "latent *beauties*" and that too, *beauties* of the *mind.*—Your definition must be incorrect. Let another try.

The Class. We cannot find out, from the connexion, what the word means, exactly; and it is useless to *guess*. Will you sir, please to tell us the meaning of it?

T. I will help you to find it out for yourselves;—you have all, I suppose, seen *unslaked lime?*

Class. Yes, sir.

2d P. You mean, I suppose, sir, limestone burnt, but not crumbled down.

T. That is exactly what is meant—it is sometimes called "*unslacked* lime"—and the pouring of water upon it, when in this condition, is called "*slacking*" it; because it slackens, or loosens the adhesion of the particles, and causes it to crumble down, or pulverizes it. For a similar reason, it seems to be called "*unslacked*" lime; and the process of pulverizing it, is called "slaking" because the water used is readily absorbed by it, and seems to quench, or slake its thirst.—But what takes place when water is poured upon a piece of lime stone that has been newly burnt?

3d. P. It grows hot.

Several of the class together—Yes, we have seen it raise a great smoke, when the masons were preparing it for mortar; and sometimes it sets the boards that are about it on fire!

T. The stone was cold; and the water still colder; where then did the heat come from that was sufficient to set a pine board on fire?

Class. We don't know.

T. Think.

4th P. It must have been either in the lime or in the water, for there was nothing else there, for the heat to come out of.

T. True, and you will be all not a little surprised when I tell you that the heat evolved, in the water.

1st P. The heat that is in water must, I think, be very well hid. One would hardly have suspected that there was heat in that which we drink when warm, because it is cold.

2d P. And I, for my part, would have been for using water, (as every body else does) to put out the fire, rather than to kindle it.

T. It is very true, that the heat which is in water, and which is set free when the water combines with the lime, *lies hid.* What kind of heat might this, then, be called?

Class. We cannot tell.

T. What word are we trying to find the meaning of?

1st P. "*Latent.*"

T. Now, what kind of heat may that about which we are arguing be called?

Class. "Latent heat!"

T. What then does the word "*latent*" mean?

1st P. It means "lying hid," for the heat was completely hid in the water.

T. We have now discovered the proper meaning of the adjective "*latent.*" Chemists tell us, that whenever a fluid becomes solid, heat is given out; and when a solid is changed into a liquid, heat is absorbed—and they call the heat which the fluid absorbs, as well as that which the solid gives out, "*latent heat;* because it is hidden or concealed in that from which it is evolved by the change. Can any of you think of any thing else that is latent? (The class is silent.)

T. You have all seen "*lightning bugs,*" or "*fire flies*" as they are sometimes called?

Class. Yes sir.

T. Do they always shine?

4th P. No, not in the day time. (a laugh somewhat at the teacher's expense.)

T. But do they constantly keep their lantern burning i
the dark?

2d P. No sir. They flash, and are dark again, and that'
the reason they are called lightning bugs.

T. But, what comes of their light between the flashes?

3d P. They hide it, sir.

Class. Then it is *"latent light"* when they conceal it.

T. Does "latent" in this case mean the same as in the cas
of the lime?

Class. Yes sir, it means hid, concealed.

T. But when this little insect darkens its lantern . . .

5th P. Then it is *rogues* lantern! (A laugh, teacher an
all.)

T. No not a rogues lantern, unless it is darkened fo
dishonest purposes. Does the lightning bug mean to b
rogueish, do you think; when he puts out his candle o
rather shuts up his lantern on the side towards the nigh
hawk or whip-poor-will?

Class. No sir.

5th P. He means to guard against rogues though.

2d P. And if *latent,* means hid, or concealed, then the fir
fly itself is latent, while he keeps his lantern dark, so far a
his enemies are concerned, whether they are whip-poor
wills, or cruel boys that might wish to destroy this tiny
torch bearer.

T. You have hit upon the very thought which I was about
to suggest, when your friend there, (pointing to the 5th
pupil,) introduced the remark about the rogues lantern.
Was it not very benevolent in the great Creator to give to
this feeble insect the means of concealing itself at will from
its pursuers?

Class. Yes, sir.

T. If you understand the meaning of the word which has
led us so long a chase, but through so pleasant a field, you
can give other illustrations of its meaning.

2d P. I think of something that is latent.

T. Then tell us what it is.

2d P. You do not know what I am thinking about.

T. No, and never should, unless you should some how or other, express your thoughts.

2d P. Well, then I guess my *thoughts* are *latent.* (a laugh). And this is like that which is said to be *latent* in the lesson—"latent beauties of the *mind,*" and thoughts not expressed, are latent in the *mind.*

T. Well said.

Several pupils together. We wish we understood all the words in the lesson, as well as we do this though it seemed at first to be the hardest.

T. You may understand not only all the words in the lesson, but all the words in the language as well, by taking the same method with each, that you have with this. Study words in their *connexion,* and you will understand them much better than by learning their definitions from a dictionary, or in an expositor. You will, it is true, find that almost every word has a variety of shades of meaning, some of which, though sanctioned by use, are not entirely correct.

No. 2.

Teacher. How is *teaching* like *training?*

Pupils. We do not very well understand what is meant by training. Solomon says in the book of Proverbs, "Train up a child in the way he should go, and when he is old he will not depart from it." But we never were sure we understood him.

T. You know what training a vine is?

1st P. It is to *direct* it right.

T. But why does it need directing?

1st P. Because it would grow in wrong directions if it were not trained or directed.

T. Does a dead vine need training?

Several of the pupils at once—No sir, because it does not grow, and therefore cannot go wrong.

T. But when a vine or any vegetable does grow, why would it go wrong if not trained?

2d P. Because it does not know how to go right, nor to take care of itself.

3d P. And if it did, it is not *strong* enough to support itself unless its tendrils were directed to something which they may take hold on, and thus support the whole vine.

T. It is best then that vines should be trained that they may not grovel on the ground, nor stray through the palings, where they might, and most probably would be trodden upon and destroyed by the mischievous and the careless. But which needs training most—the feeble or the vigorous vine?

Part of the pupils—The *feeble*—*others*, the vigorous.

T. There seems to be a difference of opinion on this subject. Let us examine it a little. *Why do you* (addressing one of the youngest who had given the first answer,) think that the *feeble* vine should have the most care taken of it? Because it is least able to take care of itself. (A pupil who had joined in the second answer.) But *taking care* is not exactly training. Besides, the luxurant vine is as much heavier in the top, as it is stronger in the stem, and needs to be held up as much as the stunted one, which if it is weak, hasn't much to carry.

2d P. And there is not much danger that the vine which doesn't grow will get *through* the palings, even if it should go in that direction.

3d P. And I remember to have heard my father say that those vines which flourished most, needed the most pruning.

1st P. But if "taking care" isn't "*training*," I wish to know whether "*pruning*" is. Does not the geranium require more care and skill to cultivate it than the night shade does? Does not the sick lamb need the most care? The youngest bird the best food? The draggled kitten the warmest place on the rug? And my little sister, because she is weak and sickly needs more care, and protection.

3d P. But does it take more to keep her out of the street or out of mischief?

All who joined in the first answer—We still think the

feeble vine most needs training—and we (quickly replied, the others) still believe the strong vine does.

T. Allow me to reconcile, if I can, your apparently different opinions. It happens to you, as to older persons, to dispute where there is really no difference of opinion. The feeble vine does need more *care,* and this a *part* of what is meant by training. This was well illustrated by reference to the geranium, the lamb, &c. But the vigorous and luxuriant vines need as much support, and more pruning than the other, all of which is also implied in training. This was well stated in the question whether the sickly little girl was more difficult to keep out of the street and out of mischief, than the more robust members of the family, who were nearly the same age? But let us not forget the question with which we set out. "What resemblance is there between teaching a child and training a vine?"

Several pupils at once—We know now.

T. Well, let us hear?

1st P. Feeble minds must be taken most care of.

2d P. And active ones will require the most guarding.

3d P. And luxuriant minds the most pruning. But, I don't think I clearly understand what can be meant by *pruning a mind.*

Several pupils together—We are sure we do not.

T. Let me explain it to you then. Those persons who are most active are in the greatest danger of going wrong, if they do not know how to go right; or are not careful to do as well as they know. They need more frequently therefore to be directed and controlled by their friends, than those who are more sluggish. These young persons, again, who have very vigorous and active minds, are like the vigorous vine whose growth is rapid, and whose branches and leaves are shooting out on all sides, so as to weigh down the stock and exhaust the vigor of the roots. Such minds are ready to stray off into a thousand unprofitable and even mischievous directions, so as to exhaust their energies, that ought to be directed to some profitable end. Such persons are full of resources and fertile in plans; but often, indeed always, in youth require the skillful bond of discipline to repress their extravagance, to guide their growth, and to lop off their redundancies.

5th P. Do then the smartest boys need the most discipline?

T. The most active and vigorous minds *often* do, but not always. Such minds are however best worth the trouble they cost. But *smart* boys are generally very *worthless*. It is the *intelligent, honest* boy, that usually rises by his modest merit to eminent usefulness.

But we have said nothing yet on the last part of the verse from Proverbs, which some of you quoted in the commencement of our conversation. What can Solomon mean, when he says that the child who is rightly trained will not depart from the right way when he is old?

3d P. I think I can tell.

T. Your class-mates will probably thank you to do so.

3d P. When a vine has become old it keeps its *set*, do as you will. You can easily turn a *green* vine another way, but when it is dried, it will break first.

5th P. But you can't make a bean vine wind round the pole in the same direction, as a hop vine does. I have tried it often, and they won't stay so a single night. One *will* wind round *with* the sun, and the other *against* the sun.

T. You are both right again, you can give any direction you please to a young vine, if it be not contrary to its *nature*. And both the kinds of vine mentioned may be trained pretty much as you please while green. But neither of them will let go their hold, when once they have been set by age. It would destroy them to be rift off.

1st P. It is plain enough then, what is meant by our not departing when we are old, from the ways in which we were *trained* while young. Old men keep on in the way in which they have gone while they were growing old—just as the old vine becomes dried in the shape which it took while it was green.

2d P. May not that be the reason why good men and bad men will never change after death?

1st P. I believe it is. You remember (addressing the teacher) you once told us that this was the force of habit.

3d P. I see it now much plainer than ever before. As long as the vine was nourished from the earth it was green and soft, though its *nature* could not be *forced*, it might be turned from its course. But when it ceased to draw its support from earth, it became fixed so that it could not be changed any more than a man's character can become vicious after he has gone to heaven.

T. Your philosophy is good, though there might be objections to your mode of stating it. But we must now close this conversation. We may resume it again should it seem best. You see of what importance it is to have the right kind of *training*, for our *characters* will certainly be such as our *habits* have been.

EXAMINATIONS.

Report on the most efficient methods of conducting examinations, in common schools, high schools, and academies

The Committee on "The Most Efficient Modes," etc., beg leave to offer the following report:

The object of education in all schools, is twofold:—first, to develop the faculties; and second, to impart knowledge.

Examinations are intended to ascertain how far these ends are attained. The best methods, then, of conducting examinations, will be those which will give the greatest assurance of arriving at correct conclusions, in regard to the fidelity of teachers, and the sound proficiency of pupils.

Examinations should be so conducted as to serve as a stimulus to all concerned in their results; and to this end, should be *fair, rigid, protracted,* and *thoroughly accurate.*

The *time* spent in preparing the lessons upon which the examinations are had, should be accurately ascertained; the amount of instruction given to each pupil, should be

carefully inquired into; and the general *character* of eac
pupil, should be rigidly scrutinized. In a word, examination
should be so conducted as to show at once the *ability* an
the *fidelity* of the instructor; and the docility, industry an
success of the learner.

To be more particular.

First. Examinations should *not* be conducted by thos
who have conducted the *recitations* of the class.

It too often happens, that there is a tacit understandin
between the teacher and his class, as to what topics shall, o
shall not come up, on examination. The class is *drilled* upon
a given number of pages, and this is taken as an intimation
of the ground over which they are to be conducted, before
the examiners and spectators; and so prompt does every
pupil become, that they are sometimes known to mortify
their teachers by answering questions before they are fairly
put. Let disinterested persons conduct the examination and
all *collusion* will be cut off.

Second. Examinations should, it is true, be conducted to
some extent, upon the same plan pursued in recitation. But
this plan, having its foundation in nature, will necessarily
suggest itself to every mind, qualified either to *examine* or
teach. It is the order of nature, to advance from *particulars*
to *generals;* to begin with examples, and end with *rules;*
and the mind of the pupil, both when receiving instruction,
and when under examination, should be directed in the road
of natural discovery. This being attended to, the greater the
diversity between the modes of recitation, and the method
pursued by the examiner, the better.

This diversity will present an old subject in a *new* light. It
will induce the pupil to believe, that he knows more of the
subject than he had supposed. It suggests to him that
neither his *author*, nor his *teacher*, nor *he* himself, had
exhausted the subject. The difference of manner between
the teacher and the examiner, may and *will* puzzle the mere
memoriter scholar—and this is one of its uses—to detect
this very vicious habit of relying on memory alone. But it
will give to the scholar whose mind has been *disciplined*, an

opportunity of displaying that mental dexterity which the *habit* of *thinking* has given him.

Third. Examinations should be extended over the whole ground occupied by the studies of the term, and each pupil should be led to expect, that he, as an *individual*, will be examined on every important principle, in the whole course of instruction, given since the last examination; and when his education is *finished*, that a *review examination* would test the accuracy of his knowledge, on *all* that he professes to have learned.

Fourth. Nothing less than this, can ensure fidelity on the part of either the teacher or the taught. Let a pupil or a preceptor know that there is a chance for escaping examination on a part of the studies of a term, and they will evince great sagacity in divining what part they will most probably be called to exhibit; and the results are—neglect of the most important parts of their studies, and an undue memoriter accuracy, or rather *flippancy* in regard to others.

Fifth. But let the teacher know that every part of the course, or of a given study, will receive a proportional attention upon examination day, and he will be more likely to take care that every part shall receive its due share of attention, during every day's recitation. And let every pupil *fear*, at least, that he will be called to give a continuous account of all that belongs to an entire subject, and he will have an additional motive, to study *each subject entire*.

Sixth. But it is easy (as easy as it is useless) to prepare a single subject well, (geography for example,) and after examination, to throw it aside, and allow it soon to be forgotten. Thus all the time and pains bestowed upon it are wasted; for it is useless to have learned *that*, whatever it may be, which we have now *forgotten*.

A few minutes more attention would often be sufficient to make an acquisition our own, with accuracy, and forever, which becomes irretrievably lost, for want of continuous thinking. Indeed a *habit* of *attention* may be formed, that without requiring more time, may make us permanently the

masters of our acquirements which a more negligen
method of study, would permit to escape.

Seventh. Examinations should be so conducted as t
ascertain *all* that has been done by both teacher and pupil

The experienced teacher will strive to combine as man
advantages as possible, in his modes of giving instruction
He will cultivate the *memory*, by requiring an accurat
recitation of numbers, dates and rules. He will cultivate th
reasoning powers, by requiring the pupil to think fo
himself, on all subjects, where his knowledge of principle
and facts is sufficient to furnish him with premises. He wil
cultivate not only his power of extemporaneous *expression*
by calling upon him to recite, without note, whole lessons
and even whole subjects, consecutively and in detail: bu'
also his powers of extempore *thinking*, by proposing
difficulties to the views he has taken, and encouraging him
at first, and afterwards *requiring* him to defend his
opinions, without previous preparation. Unless a man is
able to think without embarrassment, in any situation in
which he may probably be placed; unless he can express his
thoughts on any subject with which he is acquainted, with
accuracy, and without hesitation; unless he is able to
generalize his knowledge with rapidity, so as to construct
an argument, or defence, upon the shortest notice, he is not
educated; at least he is not educated suitably for this
country, and expecially for the West. This then, the teacher
must effect; and the business of the examiner is, to
ascertain that it has been effected.

Eighth. In order to this, let the pupil be required to recite
portions of what he has studied; without interrogation, and
without prompting. This will test his ability to express what
he knows, in his own language; the language of his author
being in no case admissible.

Again, let objections be raised to the views he has
advanced, and he be called upon to defend them. This will
exhibit his power of extempore thinking. Let him be
interrupted as he proceeds, in order to try the tenacity with
which he *retains*, and the rapidity with which he *recalls*

ideas, and trains of thought. This process, it is admitted, can have full place only in more advanced classes, and in the higher schools. But it can be approximated in every grade of instruction; and both recitations and reviews should constantly be conducted with a view to these, and such results.

Ninth. Examinations should every where be so conducted as to place the character of the school, the teacher, and the pupils in the light of truth. No deception as to *time*, accuracy, or extent of acquirement, should be left undetected or unexposed.—The object of school examinations, let it be repeated, is different from that had, in order to determine the qualifications of a teacher, or of candidates for any of the liberal professions. In the last case, it is enough to know the extent of a man's qualifications, irrespective of the time spent in the acquisition.—But in the other, *periodical* examinations are had in order to ascertain the progress of the school, in a given time. Nothing, it is believed, will be so efficient in bringing a press of motive always to bear upon both teacher and pupil, as the certain anticipation of a full, fair and thorough examination, on all that has been done during the whole term intervening between examinations.

Tenth. Examinations should be so conducted as to exhibit *all* the results of education, to whatever point it may have progressed. In order to do this, the examiners should carefully note every indication of mental development, and moral improvement. These will be manifested in a greater variety of ways than might, at first, be suspected; and certainly in a much greater variety than can be here laid down. The deportment of the pupils, toward their instructors, examiners, and among themselves, will furnish *one* criterion. The order of movement, and the state of the furniture in the school-room, will furnish another. The *mechanical* execution of the task assigned, whether on the blackboard, the slate, or on paper, may be considered as a third.

Extempore compositions—by which is meant, essays written by a whole class upon a topic suggested by the examiners, without time for previous reflection, or any aid from grammars, dictionaries, common place books, or authors—might serve as a fourth.

In a word, as education aims at making a man what he *ought* to *be*, and furnishing him with an acquaintance with all that he ought to *know;* examinations should be so conducted, as to exhibit all the effects of discipline, instruction, and education—the formation of habits—the acquisition of knowledge, and the building up of character. When this shall be done, examinations will be very different in their character and uses from what they have too often hitherto been.

ANALYSIS
OF
THE ENGLISH ALPHABET.

LETTERS are characters made to represent sounds. Syllables are formed of letters; words are formed of syllables. There are twenty-six letters in the English language, namely: A, B, C, D, E, F, G, H, I, J, K ,L ,M, N, O, P, Q, R, S, T, U, V, W, X, Y, Z. These letters taken together are called the English Alphabet.

The ALPHABET is divided into VOWELS and CONSONANTS. A VOWEL is a letter which can be sounded by itself, without the use of another letter.

The VOWELS are A, E, I, O, U, W; Y is sometimes a vowel and sometimes a consonant.

NOTE.—It has been customary to consider W a consonant when it commences a word; but Doct. Webster, with apparent reason, claims that it is always a vowel. It surely answers the usual definition of a vowel, viz: "a letter which can be sounded by itself;" and agrees closely in pronunciation with the OU of the French, and the U of the Spanish.

The CONSONANTS are B, C, D, F, G, H, J, K, L, M, N, P, Q, R, S, T, V, X, Z, and sometimes Y.

QUESTIONS. What do letters represent? Of what are syllables formed? How many letters are there in the English alphabet? What are they? How is the alphabet divided? What is a vowel? Repeat the vowels. Repeat the consonants. What letter is both a vowel and a consonant?

DIPHTHONGS AND TRIPHTHONGS.

In every syllable there must be at least one vowel. When two vowels are united in one sound, so as to form one syllable, their union is called a diphthong; as OU in *loud*; EA in *ea-ger*.

The union of three vowels in one syllable it called a triphthong; as IEU in *lieu*.

A *pure* diphthong is one in which the sounds of both vowels are united; as OI in *voice, oil.*

An *impure* diphthong is one in which one of the vowels only is sounded; as AI in *aim.*

There are four pure diphthongs; OI, OY, OU, and OW; as in *toil, boy, round, cow*; OU and OW are sometimes impure, as in *tough, low.*

The impure diphthongs in common use, are AE, AI, AU, AW, AY, EA, EI, EO, EU, EW, EY, IA, IE, OA, OE, OO, UA, UE, UI: as in *seal, autumn, coal, bread, sail, say, either, yeoman, people*, &c.

QUESTIONS. What is a diphthong? A triphthong? What is a pure diphthong? An impure diphthong? Give examples of words in which there are pure diphthongs. Give examples of words in which there are impure diphthongs. Give examples of triphthongs.

SOUNDS OF THE VOWELS.

A has four sounds; lst, a long sound, as in fate;^{1} 2d, a flat sound, as in far;^{2} 3d, a broad sound, as in fall, what;^{3} ^{3} 4th, a short sound, as in f at.^{4}

NOTE.—The difference between the sounds of A in *fall* and *what,* are deemed too nice to be appreciated by an unpracticed ear, and therefore no distinction has been made between them in this table. The same thing may be said with regard to the sounds of O in *nor* and *not*; and of U, in *rule* and *tube.*

G has two sounds; hard, as in *gave*; soft, as in *gem.*
When marked with the cedilla (ģ), it is soft.

H is but a forcible breathing before the following vowel. It is silent after R, as in *rhyme*. When preceded by W. it is sounded before it, as in *when*, (pronounced *hwen*.)

J has the sound of G soft, as in *Jane*. In *hallelujah*, it takes the sound of Y.

K has but one sound, as in *kind*.

L has one sound, as in *live*. It is often silent when followed by another consonant, as in *calm*.

M, N, P, Q and R have one sound each, as in *man*, *not*, *pit*, *question*, *run*. Q is always followed by U; *together, they are pronounced like KW, as in quite*, pronounced *kwite*.

S has a soft sound, as in *set*, and the sound of Z, as in *rise*. When marked with a cedilla (ş) it has the sound of Z.

T and V have one sound each, as in *tin*, *vice*.

X has the sound of KS, as in *wax*; and of GS, as in *exact*; and of Z, as in *Xenophon*.

Y and Z have one sound each, as in *yes*, *zinc*.

QUESTIONS. How are consonants divided? What are mutes? Name them. What are semi-vowels? Name them. What are liquids? Name them.

NOTE.—The teacher will find it highly advantageous to question the pupil *minutely* and *carefully*, on the above table of consonant sounds, calling for examples, &c.

DOUBLE CONSONANTS.

Ch have the sound nearly of *tsh*, as in *church*; of *k*, as in *chorus*, and of *sh*, as in *chaise*.

Gh are generally mute; when pronounced, they take the sound of G hard, as in *ghost*, or of F, as in *tough*.

Ph have the sound of F, as in *philosophy*.

Sh have but one sound, as in *ship*.

Th have an aspirate sound, as in *think*; or hard, as in *thou*.

FINAL SYLLABLES.

The final syllables *cean, cion, sion, tion,* have the
sound of *shun*, as in *ocean, suspicion, version,
commotion.*

Ceous, cious, scious, tious, have the sound of *shus*;
as in *cetaceous, gracious, conscious, cautious.*

Cian, tian, have the sound of *shan*, as in *magician,
gentian.*

Cial, sial, tial, have the sound of *shl*, as in *social,
ambrosial, partial.*

Science, tience, have the sound of *shense*, as in
conscience, patience.

QUESTIONS. What is the sound of the final
syllables, *cean, cion, sion, tion?* Give examples. What
is the sound of *ceous, cious, scious, tious?* Of *cian,
tian?* Of *cial, sial, tial?* Of *science, tience?* Give examples of each of the above.

REVIEW.

Repeat the letters of the Alphabet. How is the
Alphabet divided? How many vowels are there? What
are they? What letter is both a vowel and a consonant? What do you call the union of two vowels in
one syllable? What the union of three vowels? Repeat
the table of the vowel sounds, and give examples.
What are mutes? Repeat them. What are semi-
vowels? What are liquids? What are some of the
double consonants, and how are they sounded? Can
you give examples of the irregular sounds of the
vowels?

DISCOVER THE AMAZING DIFFERENCE!

1836-1837 EDITIONS

ORIGINAL McGUFFEY'S ECLECTIC Readers

THERE WAS A DIFFERENCE!

Few people today are aware of the *significant difference* between the original **Eclectic Readers** written by Rev. William H. McGuffey in 1836-1837 and the watered-down revisions of 1857 and 1879.

Although they bear the McGuffey name, the later revisions *secularized* the earlier **Eclectic Readers** by removing passages concerning faith in Jesus Christ, piety, theology, virtue, morality, and Christian spiritual growth.

McGuffey's family migrated to America in the late 1700's. Like many others, they came armed with a strong Faith in God and a desire to establish religious communities. They were pious pioneers who battled the hardships of frontier life. It was this spiritual environment which produced William Holmes McGuffey.

McGuffey invested his life in two pursuits: education and preaching the Gospel. He was a master at integrating the acquisition of learning skills with the building of strong moral character.

In 1836 he published the first of his **Eclectic Readers**. The Original **Readers** were filled with stories of strength and character, of goodness and truth, of God, Christ, and the Bible. William H. McGuffey always emphasized the scriptural truths in his stories.

READ THE ORIGINAL STORIES WHICH:
- Built strong character
- Reinforced positive moral development
- Displayed quality examples of Christian citizenship
- Contained stories of
        —truth and goodness
        —courage and determination
        —faith and forgiveness
        —kindness and obedience
        —patience and service
        —gratefulness and wisdom

THESE ORIGINAL McGUFFEY READERS
provide concrete examples of right living . . . they will not be forgotten!

RETURN TO THE BASICS . . .
*readin', 'riting, 'rithemetic,
and religious convictions!*

PUT GODLY PRINCIPLES BACK INTO YOUR PRIORITIES!

THE DIFFERENCE IS SIGNIFICANT!

Not only is it important to realize that Rev. William H. McGuffey did not write the **McGuffey Readers** which are currently available, but none of the *original* edition's emphasis on piety and salvation are found in them.

The spirit of self-reliance, individualism and competition fill the pages of the 1879 edition: "Virtue is rarely its own reward, but material and physical rewards can be expected for good acts . . . responsibility for success and failure lies with the individual."

There are no stories of rebels, reformers, dissenters, pilgrims, or seekers in these later editions.

Read for yourself of the areas of difference . . .

William Holmes McGuffey—teacher, preacher, college president, writer, educational reformer, and schoolbook compiler—is perhaps the most important figure in the history of American public education, yet very few people know much about the man himself. Except for a few letters, a pair of handwritten sermons and one unpublished manuscript on moral philosophy, his known writings are few.

In addition to using the Readers to teach students to read and to spell, McGuffey also sought to build character and to instill Christian values through them.

A Biographical Note
on
The Reverend Doctor John H. Westerhoff, III

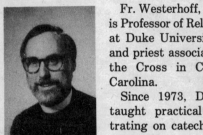

Fr. Westerhoff, an Episcapal priest, is Professor of Religion and Education at Duke University Divinity School and priest associate at the Chapel of the Cross in Chapel Hill, North Carolina.

Since 1973, Dr. Westerhoff has taught practical theology, concentrating on catechetics, liturgics and spirituality.

Author of more than fifteen books and numerous articles, he is editor of *Religious Education*, an international, ecumenical, scholarly journal of the Religious Education Association and the Association of Professors and Researchers in Religious Education.

He has earned his graduate degrees in theology, anthropology and education from Harvard and Columbia University. A world-wide lecturer, he spent his first eight years in parish ministry, followed by eight years in a denominational education office and most recently as a divinity school professor having taught at Harvard, Fordham University, Boston College, The University of the South, Princeton, General and Union Theological Seminary.

His most recent books are *Will Our Children Have Faith?*; *Bringing Up Children in the Christian Faith*; *A Faithful Church: Issues in the History of Catechesis*; *Christian Believing*; *Liturgy and Learning through the Life Cycle*; *Inner Growth/Outer Change*; and *The Spiritual Life: Learning East and West*.

He and his wife Barnie live in Durham, North Carolina. They have three children, Jill, Jack, and Beth.

DISCOVER
THE DIFFERENCE
FOR YOURSELF . . .

ORDER YOUR
PERSONAL SET TODAY!

Yes! I'm convinced . . . Send me a set today!

Name _____ Date _____

Address _____ Phone _____

City _____ State _____ Zip _____

☐ Check enclosed # _____

Charging Your Order?

☐ Master Charge   ☐ Bank Americard

Card No. _____

Expires _____

Bank I.D. (Master Charge only _____)

Signature _____

Send to: **Mott Media, Inc.**
1000 East Huron Street
Milford, Michigan 48042

Regular Price $69.95

Introductory offer $49.95

Save $20 OFFER ENDS
DEC. 1, 1982

(Please Add $3.00 for
postage and Handling)

Or Call: 1-800-521-4350
[In Michigan Call]
(313) 685-8773]

---------- Clip and Send ----------

216

DISCOVER
THE DIFFERENCE
FOR YOURSELF . . .

ORDER YOUR
PERSONAL SET TODAY!

Yes! I'm convinced . . . Send me a set today!

Name _____

Address _____

City _____ State _____

Date _____

Phone _____

Zip _____

☐ Check enclosed # _____

Charging Your Order?

☐ Master Charge   ☐ Bank Americard

Card No. _____

Expires _____

Bank I.D. (Master Charge only _____)

Signature _____

Send to: **Mott Media, Inc.**
1000 East Huron Street
Milford, Michigan 48042

Regular Price $69.95

Introductory offer $49.95

Save $20   OFFER ENDS
DEC. 1, 1982

(Please Add $3.00 for
postage and Handling)

Or Call: 1-800-521-4350
[In Michigan Call]
(313) 685-8773]

-------- Clip and Send --------

DISCOVER
THE DIFFERENCE
FOR YOURSELF ...

ORDER YOUR
PERSONAL SET TODAY!

Yes! I'm convinced . . . Send me a set today!

Name _____ Date _____

Address _____ Phone _____

City _____ State _____ Zip _____

☐ Check enclosed #

Charging Your Order?

☐ Master Charge   ☐ Bank Americard

Card No. _____

Expires _____

Bank I.D. (Master Charge only _____)

Signature _____

Send to: **Mott Media, Inc.**
1000 East Huron Street
Milford, Michigan 48042

Regular Price $69.95

Introductory offer $49.95

Save $20 OFFER ENDS
DEC. 1, 1982

(Please Add $3.00 for
postage and Handling)

Or Call: 1-800-521-4350
[In Michigan Call]
(313) 685-8773]

DISCOVER THE DIFFERENCE FOR YOURSELF ...

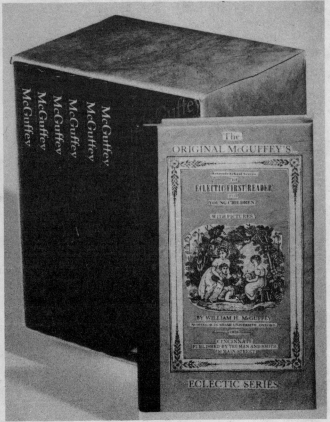

ORDER YOUR PERSONAL SET TODAY!

Yes! I'm convinced . . . Send me a set today!

Name _____ Date _____

Address _____ Phone _____

City _____ State _____ Zip _____

☐ Check enclosed #

Charging Your Order?

☐ Master Charge   ☐ Bank Americard

Card No. _____

Expires _____

Bank I.D. (Master Charge only _____)

Signature _____

Send to: **Mott Media, Inc.**
1000 East Huron Street
Milford, Michigan 48042

Regular Price $69.95

Introductory offer $49.95   OFFER ENDS
DEC. 1, 1982

Save $20

(Please Add $3.00 for
postage and Handling)

Or Call: 1-800-521-4350
[In Michigan Call]
(313) 685-8773]

-------- Clip and Send --------

DISCOVER
THE DIFFERENCE
FOR YOURSELF...

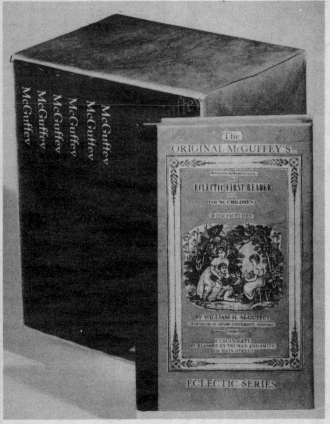

ORDER YOUR
PERSONAL SET TODAY!

Yes! I'm convinced . . . Send me a set today!

Name _____ Date _____

Address _____ Phone _____

City _____ State _____ Zip _____

☐ Check enclosed # _____

Charging Your Order?

☐ Master Charge   ☐ Bank Americard

Card No. _____

Expires _____

Bank I.D. (Master Charge only _____)

Signature _____

Send to: **Mott Media, Inc.**
1000 East Huron Street
Milford, Michigan 48042

Regular Price $69.95

Introductory offer **$49.95**

Save $20   OFFER ENDS
DEC. 1, 1982

(Please Add $3.00 for
postage and Handling)

Or Call: 1-800-521-4350
[In Michigan Call]
(313) 685-8773]

-------- Clip and Send --------